BOOK NUMBERS
History, Principles, and Application

DONALD J. LEHNUS

American Library Association/Chicago 1980

D0807510

Library of Congress Cataloging in Publication Data

Lehnus, Donald J   1934–
  Book numbers.

  "Bibliography of Cutter author number
tables": p.
  Bibliography: p.
  Includes index.
  1. Shelf-listing (Library science) I. Title.
Z698.L425   025.4'2   80–23100
ISBN 0–8389–0316–9

Printed in the United States of America

Contents

PART ONE

Historical Background

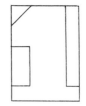

Introduction
and Definitions

A library is more than just a mere "book collection" because it has a systematic organization which permits the identification and location of specific items. This systematic organization is the result of cataloging and classification. An important factor in the organization of a library's materials is a group of symbols used to indicate the location of each item; this group of symbols is termed "call number." The call number is always found in the upper left-hand corner of catalog cards and consists of two basic elements: (1) the classification number, and (2) the book number (also called "author number" or "cutter number"). This group of symbols determines the arrangement of the materials not only by topic, but also by a systematic subarrangement. The call number serves as a finding device for any specific item. The classification number indicates the subject of the book according to the classification scheme used by the library, thus organizing in one place all the materials on the same topic. The book number subarrangès and determines an orderly and logical position for each item assigned the same classification number. Examples of call numbers:

```
973.7 ←――――――― Classification number ―――――――→  574
B652  ←――――――― Book number ―――――――――――――――→  P483t
              Work mark ―――――――――――――――――――――↑
```

The groups of symbols used to indicate the location of a specific item plays an important role in finding library materials. Everyone who looks for materials in a library, whether he or she is a professional librarian or a first-time library user, must depend on these symbols to locate any specific desired item.

To have a thorough understanding of the important role played by book numbers in the organization of library materials it is necessary to be familiar with the terminology used in this facet of the classification process. The following definitions of the basic terminology are from four authoritative sources.[1] After each definition there is an indication showing from which of the four sources the definition was taken.

Call Number

1. Call number—letters, figures, and symbols, separate or in combination, assigned to a book to indicate its location on shelves. It usually consists of class number and book number. Sometimes known as Call Mark. (ALA, p. 22)
2. Call-mark—characters indicating the location of a book on the shelves and distinguishing it from all others in the library. Usually composed of class number and book number. (Cutter, p. 14)
3. Call number—a combination of characters assigned to a library book to indicate its place on the shelf relative to other books. (Webster's, p. 319)
4. Call number—the notation used to identify and locate a particular book on the shelves; it consists of the classification number and author number, and it may also include a work number (work mark). (Wynar, p. 402)

Classification Number

1. Class number—a number used to designate a specific division of a classification scheme whose notation consists wholly or in part of numerals. (ALA, p. 30)
2. Class-mark—one or more characters showing the class to which a book belongs. In a relative location this also shows its place on the shelves. (Cutter, p. 17)
3. Class number—a number or letter (from a classification scheme)

---

1. *A.L.A. glossary of library terms, with a selection of terms in related fields* (Chicago: American Library Association, 1943, Charles A. Cutter, *Rules for a dictionary catalog*, 4th ed., rewritten (Washington: Government Printing Office, 1904); *Webster's third new international dictionary of the English language*, Unabr. (Springfield, Mass.: G. & C. Merriam Company, 1976); Bohdan S. Wynar, *Introduction to cataloging and classification*, 5th ed. prepared with the assistance of John Phillip Immroth (Littleton, Col.: Libraries Unlimited, 1976).

assigned to a book or other library material to show its location on the library shelf. (Webster's, p. 417)

4. Classification number—the number assigned to an item of a collection to show the subject area and to indicate its location on the library shelf. (Wynar, p. 403)

Book Number

1. Author number—a combination of letters and figures assigned to each book for the purpose of preserving on the shelves an alphabetical arrangement by author under each class. (ALA, p. 9)
2. Book number—a combination of letters and figures used to arrange books in the same classification number in alphabetical order. It usually consists of an author number and a work mark. Occasionally called Book Mark. (ALA, p. 16)
3. Cutter number—an author number from one of the Cutter tables or from the Cutter-Sanborn 3-figure Alphabetic Table. (ALA, p. 42)
4. Book number—one or more characters, used to distinguish an individual book from all others having the same class, shelf, or other generic number. (Cutter, p. 14)
5. Author number, also author mark—a character or characters representing an author's surname in a call number. (Webster's, p. 147)
6. Book number—a combination of letters and figures used to distinguish an individual book from all others having the same library classification number. (Webster's, p. 253)
7. Cutter number—a combination of characters representing an author's surname, composed of the initial letter followed by numbers (as M62 = Milne, M64 = Milton), chosen to make the numerical order of the symbols correspond to the alphabetical order of the names, and used to arrange books in the same class alphabetically by authors. (Webster's, p. 562)
8. Book number—the symbols, usually a combination of letters and numbers, used to distinguish books with the same classification number in order to maintain the alphabetical order (by author) of books on the shelves; also called an author number. Cutter number is another term used, deriving from the widespread use of Cutter-Sanborn tables to devise book number symbols. (Wynar, p. 402)

Work Mark

1. Work mark—the part of a book number that distinguishes one title from other titles by the same author when the books have the same

class number. Sometimes called Title Mark or Title Letter. (ALA, p. 150)

2. Title mark—that part of the book mark which is used to distinguish different books by the same author. (Cutter, p. 24)
3. Work mark—a letter (or letters) placed after the cutter number. A work mark may consist of one or two letters, the first of which is the first letter of the title of a work (exclusive of articles). Also called work number. (Wynar, p. 411)

To Cutter

The use of "cutter" as a verb (to assign a Cutter number to [Webster's, p. 562]) has become quite acceptable in library literature and since the definition appears in Webster's dictionary its use is supported and condoned. The Library of Congress *Cataloging Service Bulletin* frequently uses it as a verb (e.g., Bulletin 116, Winter 1976, p. 6; and Bulletin 120, Winter 1977, p. 16). John Immroth in his *A guide to the Library of Congress classification* also used it as a verb (e.g., p. 49 of the second edition).

From the above definitions of "book number" it is obvious that the terms "author number" and "cutter number" are often used synonymously. Cutter number is a precise eponym when one of the Cutter tables is used, or if the term is used to honor Charles A. Cutter for his role in the development of book numbers as they are known today. However, the use of cutter number instead of book number does not take into consideration the work mark or other letters and/or figures which often form part of the book number, and are not derived from a Cutter table. Author number is commonly used because the number is often formed from the author's name, but with the current and ever growing trend in cataloging to use the title as the main entry for so many different types of works this term is not precise. Book numbers may be formed from titles and/or the name of a person or entity connected with the production of a publication, and also often contain elements that are not related to the author, such as editors, compilers, illustrators, translators, publishers, and the year of publication. Because of these various elements which may be included, the term "book number" is more inclusive and exact, and therefore the most appropriate term.

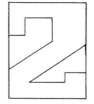

Origins

During the last quarter of the nineteenth century the field of librarianship advanced further and had more developments than in the preceding four centuries after the invention of the printing press. Among these advances were the creation of classification schemes and the formulation of book numbering plans. Librarians of this period were making classification systems and advocating the classification of library materials by subjects rather than the assigning of fixed location symbols and shelving books in fixed places. In a small pamphlet published in 1882, for the users of the Boston Athenaeum, Charles A. Cutter explained in layman's terms why that library began to classify the books rather than assign them fixed location symbols as had been done in the past. He describes the advantages of classification by writing:

EXPLANATION OF THE NEW SYSTEM OF

MARKING BOOKS

As some persons have shown a desire to know more about the new way of numbering than was strictly necessary for getting the books, I have prepared a brief explanation of the most prominent points, in order to answer at once many questions; but it is not necessary to remember or even to understand this explanation in order to use the library.

REASONS FOR MAKING THE CHANGE

The greater part of the shelves having become inconveniently full, some of them bearing double and some triple rows of books, and a new room having been shelved with a capacity for 50,000 volumes, it became necessary to rearrange the whole library. That implies putting new place marks on the catalogues, a work which, as it requires the greatest care to avoid errors (for a book mismarked is practically a book lost), would certainly take a long time and be expensive. And yet there is not the consolation of feeling that what is done is to be of permanent value. Our past experience shows that it would all have to be done over again within a dozen years, when, with a larger library, the task would be still more expensive. It is therefore plainly expedient to abandon the antiquated system which makes this decennial change of shelf marks necessary, and to adopt a method which will allow the books to be moved hereafter, whenever **necessary**, without any change of the marks on the catalogues. This can be effected by making the book-numbers indicate not a given alcove and shelf, but a given class and sub-class, and if necessary, sub-sub-class; so that a book-number once correctly assigned will remain unchanged forever, although the place of the book be changed a hundred times; and, consequently, the cost and loss of time and liability to mistakes inherent in the other plan, will be done away with at once. For instance, it is plain that a History of England should always have the class-number assigned to English histories (8E), no matter in what part of the building that class may be placed. And any number of new works may come into that class, yet its subject-number or letter will be unaltered.

The old method may be compared to the line in the directory which states that a man lives at 129 Grace Street; the method proposed may be compared to the army register, which says that he is captain of Company C, 5th Regiment, M.V.M. Let the regiment be marched all over the country, yet the soldier is easily found by his position in it. If the citizen moves to a new street, a new directory is needed, but the army register does not have to be altered whenever the regiment is quartered in a different town. Similarly, books may be found by their position in a certain class, though the class itself be transferred from one alcove to another, or from one building to another.

A second improvement was much needed. In the old system books are marked merely to alcove and shelf, an insufficient practice, to be found in hardly any other library of importance in the country. When one had reached the right shelf, one was far from having found one's book. It was still necessary to hunt it up, by its title, among the often badly lettered volumes, on the often ill-lighted shelf. In the new system, every book has a definite place in its section, and the mark which determines that place is legibly stamped on the back. Thus, as in other American libraries, every volume has its own mark, shared with no other volume, its proper name, by which it is absolutely identified, and by which it can be quickly and safely described in any of the operations of library management.[1]

The application of classification schemes to library collections brought about a systematic and logical, as well as a practical arrangement of books

1. Charles Ammi Cutter, *Boston Athenaeum: How to get books, with an explanation of the new way of marking books* (Boston: Press of Rockwell and Churchill, 1882), pp. 6–7.

according to subjects. Therefore, it is only natural that the librarians of this period who were concerned with the organization of collections would soon realize the need for an equally systematic and logical, as well as a practical subarrangement of the materials under each classification number, which at the same time would provide each item with a unique call number.

Those who were devising classification systems also began to invent various methods of subarranging individual items under each classification number. However, the actual evolution of book numbers was independent of any classification scheme even though they were coeval. There are five librarians who stand out as the most important and influential in the evolution of book numbers. These five are:

1. Jacob Schwartz (1846–1926), librarian of the New York Apprentices' Library from 1871 to 1900.
2. Charles Ammi Cutter (1837–1903), librarian of the Boston Athenaeum from 1868 to 1893, and librarian at the Forbes Library in Northampton, Massachusetts from 1894 to 1903.
3. Melvil Dewey (1851–1931), the "father of modern librarianship"; assistant at the Amherst College library from 1873 to 1876; editor of *Library journal* and secretary of the American Library Association from 1876 to 1883; founder of the Readers and Writers Economy Company, Library Bureau, and the Spelling Reform Association; president of the American Metric Bureau; from 1883 to 1889 librarian of Columbia College where he founded the first library school; director of the New York State Library in Albany, from 1889 to 1905.
4. John Edmands (1820–1915), librarian of the Mercantile Library of Philadelphia from 1856 to 1901.
5. Kate Emery Sanborn Jones (1860–1951), cataloger at the Boston Athenaeum from 1883 to 1891; cataloger at the Mercantile Library in St. Louis from 1891 to 1894; and librarian of the Manchester (N.H.) Public Library from 1894 to 1897.

Charles A. Cutter, who played a major role in the development of book numbers, was also the first to point out their origin. In 1882 he wrote:

```
Alphabetical arrangement of a whole library in one alphabet,

and alphabetical arrangement of the two special subjects, Fiction

and Biography, have long been in practice; but M. J. Schwartz, of

the Apprentices' Library of New York, was the first, so far as I

know, to arrange alphabetically all of the sections of a minutely
```

```
subdivided library.  He certainly was the first to maintain this

order by the use of a table in which the names were represented

by numbers.  (See Library journal 3:6-10.)   His table, however,

was made on an entirely different principle from mine, the integral

numbers from 1 to 99 being assigned to combinations of letters

from Aaa to Zyz.  The idea of using a table of decimal fractions,

so as to be able to make intercalations ad infinitum, is my own.

Prefixing to these fractions the initial of the author is an idea

borrowed from Mr. J: Edmands, of the Mercantile Library of Phila-

delphia, who has made an author table on a principle differing

from both Mr. Schwartz's and mine, but, like Mr. Schwartz's,

not designed for intercalation.[2]
```

Jacob Schwartz "rearranged," that is, recataloged and reclassified, the collection of the New York Apprentices' Library in 1872. Schwartz used his own classification system, called the "Combined" classification system, that is, combined alphabetical and numerical system. He also devised an author table to be used to subarrange the materials by author under each classification number. In an article in the March 1878 issue of *Library journal*, Schwartz described the classification system and the author table that accompanied it. Schwartz stated that he had devised his system early in 1871 and used it in rearranging the New York Apprentices' Library in 1872. His author table subarranged the materials not only by the author's surname, but also according to the size, that is, height of the book. Schwartz's reasons for the size arrangement were, first, to give the books an orderly and aesthetic appearance, and secondly and principally to economize space and facilitate delivery to readers.

Schwartz's classification system consisted of twenty-five general divisions, each designated by a letter of the alphabet, A to Z, excluding J. Under each letter there were nine subclasses indicated by the digits, 1 to 9, and each of these subclasses could be further divided by the twenty-five letters, a to z, excluding j. Within each division, whether it be the general class, subclass, or sub-subclass, the books were first distributed according to size. Four size groups were used and each book was measured and categorized as a duodecimo, an octavo, a quarto, or a folio. Schwartz created a table in which the

2. Ibid. pp. 35–36.

numbers 0 to 999 were divided among the four sizes: duodecimos, 0 to 499; octavos, 500 to 799; quartos, 800 to 899; and folios, 900 to 999. This table was based on the assumption that in every hundred books there are an average of 50 duodecimos, 30 octavos, 10 quartos, and 10 folios. Within each size the books were arranged alphabetically by author or by title when there was no known author and assigned a number according to its position in the alphabet, that is, A would have the lowest number and Z the highest. These numbers representing the author or title were appended to the classification number and were indistinguishable from it. The letter R stood for the category "European history and travels" and was followed by a digit representing a particular country, and then the number representing the size and the author or title was appended to the classification number, that is:

```
Kohlrausch.   History of Germany   (octavo)      R.4651

Wyndam.       German history       (octavo)      R.4796
```

The first digit represents Germany and the last three stand for the author's name. If the book by Kohlrausch had been a duodecimo the classification number would be R.4252; if it were a quarto the number would be R.4851; a folio, R.4951. Thus the last three digits arrange the books first by size and subarrange them alphabetically.[3]

Just six months after Schwartz had presented his book numbering plan, Cutter commented on Schwartz's book numbers and also expressed disapproval of Melvil Dewey's way of simply supplying a sequential accession number to each book with the same classification number. Cutter indicated that decimal numbers used as book numbers would allow for the intercalation of materials without disturbing the alphabetical subarrangement by author. In the article Cutter pointed out that Dewey's system of sequentially numbering the books would give only a chronological arrangement according to the date of acquisition of the materials. This might be useful if only new books were acquired in the order in which they are published, but libraries acquire old books as well as new ones, and even the new ones are not cataloged in a chronological order of publication date. Therefore, Cutter felt that Dewey's sequential accession numbers furnished no logical order under each classification number. Cutter suggested that book numbers should be decimal numbers to permit indefinite interpolation. He presented tables and stated that authors should be distinguished entirely by numbers, reserving letters to mark different books by the same author. The following tables show Cutter's original thinking on the idea of author numbers:

3. Jacob Schwartz, *"A 'combined' system for arranging and numbering,"* *Library journal* 3 (March 1878): 6–8.

Divide the alphabet into ten parts.

A-Bo 0		M 5
Br-C 1		N-R 6
D-F 2		S 7
G-H 3		T-V 8
I-L 4		W-Z 9

In a class containing very few books even this table would
suffice; thus a book by Cleveland would be numbered 1;
Damoureau, 2; Goupil, 3, and so on; but when a book by Gray
came into that class it would be necessary to subdivide 3 thus:

Ga-Gik 30	Hay-Heq 35
Gil-Goq 31	Her-Hik 36
Gor-Guk 32	Hil-Hoe 37
Gul-Ham 33	Hof-Hor 38
Han-Hax 34	Hu-Hz 39

According to this second table, while Goupil remains 3, Gray ·
becomes 32. This table gives us 100 numbers for a subclass, which
is enough for most. But if a book should come in written by
Gordon, we must subdivide 32 as we did 3, thus:

Gor-Got 320	Gri-Gril 325
Gou-Gral 321	Grim-Griz 326
Gram-Graz 322	Gro-Gru 327
Gre-Grel 323	Gry-Gub 328
Grem-Grez 324	Guc-Guk 329

We should then have

Goupil 3

Gray 32

Gordon 320

which is not strictly alphabetical. Two things may then be

done. Either the names can be renumbered and all three have their exacter equivalent,

       Gordon 320

       Goupil 321

       Gray 322

or the precise alphabetical order can be disregarded. As very great accuracy is in this matter of little account, the latter course would generally be best, until the class becomes large, when a readjustment of little tangles of this sort would become necessary....

       Of course the numbers, being decimal fractions, succeed each other like the letters in a dictionary, that is, 1, 12, 13, 135, 1354, 136, 14, not 1, 12, 13, 14, 135, 136, 1354; and if a book comes in that should go between 12 and 13, it will be so arranged if it receives the number 121....[4]

Cutter did not like Schwartz's idea of incorporating the author number into the classification number without any distinction as to where one ended and the other began, and considered that it was necessary to set apart the book number from the classification number. He also commented that libraries might prefer to use the author's name instead of a book number, using only as many letters of the name as needed to distinguish it from the preceding book and the following one. However, Cutter did believe that there were advantages in using book numbers because they are more easily written and read, and easier to arrange by.

Schwartz was not in accord with Cutter and expressed the view that Cutter's ideas of decimal author numbers were too detailed and would only be useful in very large libraries, because as he pointed out, he had never had any problems with his system. Schwartz prided himself in the fact that his scheme required at the most only four digits in addition to two class letters, and a letter representing the title, and claimed that these would be sufficient to classify at least 100,000,000 volumes. He believed that it was a serious

4. Charles Ammi Cutter, "Another plan for numbering books," *Library journal* 3 (September 1878): 249–51.

mistake to plan an elaborate classification scheme, because the divisions of a scheme should be proportioned to the number of books in a given library, and that subdivisions should only be used as the need for them might arise.[5]

A library symposium on book numbers was published in the February 1879 issue of *Library journal* and consisted of contributions by: John Edmands, Mercantile Library of Philadelphia; Josephus N. Larned, Young Men's Association's Library of Buffalo, New York, (later the name was changed to Buffalo Library); Melvil Dewey, editor of *Library journal*; Charles A. Cutter, Boston Athenaeum; and Frederic B. Perkins, Boston Public Library. It was in this symposium that John Edmands proposed a plan to use the initial letter of the author's surname followed by digits to represent the other letters of the name. Edmands is the first person known to have publicly expressed this idea of combining the initial letter with numbers.

Edmands arranged all books in alphabetical order, first by the name of the author and then by title under each author. The initial letter of the author's last name was followed by digits and immediately below it a number was used to designate that particular title, that is: Dickens' *Oliver Twist*, $\frac{D420}{61}$; Trollope's *Barchester Towers*, $\frac{T730}{15}$. For some reason Edmands believed that confusion would result if certain letters of the alphabet were used, so the letters J, P, V, and Y were substituted for I, Q, U, X, and Z. Therefore, Irving's *Sketch-book* was given the number, $\frac{J240}{50}$. Edmands pointed out that his system was superior to any other then in use because (1) the books on the shelves formed their own catalog, (2) the scheme kept all the books by one author in one place, (3) the possibility of expansion was provided, and (4) it could be easily understood and applied.[6]

In the same symposium Melvil Dewey criticized several factors of Edmands's plan. Dewey had carefully analyzed the ideas put forth by Schwartz, Cutter, and Edmands, and was convinced that the basic idea of "author numbers" was well worth experimenting with. He hoped that after his experiments he would be better able to decide if it would be worthwhile to translate names into numbers. Dewey totally disagreed with Edmands's idea of using J, P, V, and Y instead of I, Q, U, X, and Z and commented that this would be more confusing than an occasional error when one of these letters might be mistaken for another. But, he did favor Schwartz's basic idea of translating names into numbers, and agreed that the best order under a

---

5. Jacob Schwartz, "Mr. Cutter's numbering plan," *Library journal* 3 (October 1878): 302.

6. John Edmands, "Plans for numbering, with especial reference to fiction : a library symposium," *Library journal* 4 (February 1879): 38–40.

classification number was the alphabetical arrangement by authors and by titles under authors.[7]

Cutter's initial response to Edmands's use of the initial letter combined with numbers was negative. Cutter believed that the use of a letter made an "insignificant gain" and that a mixture of letters and numbers was "objectionable." Cutter had examined library catalogs and brought out the fact that it was not uncommon that catalogs contain several persons with the same last name and that it would require a much shorter author number to distinguish them if only numbers were used. He expressed the opinion that he did prefer letters for "class notation," and numbers for the "author notation." He preferred numbers for the "author notation" because their superiority in ease of writing, reading, remembering, and arranging would compensate for their inferior capacity, which is of less importance in author numbers than in classification numbers. However, he finally concluded by confessing that he was not sure which system he might finally decide upon.[8]

In his response to Cutter's contribution to the symposium Dewey professed Edmands's plan to be superior and endorsed it with the following comments:

```
If adopting a translation system I should follow Mr. Edmands
in using the author's initial and translating only the rest of
his name.  This helps the memory greatly and increases the capacity
of the first character 26, thus often saving a figure.  The objec-
tion to having both letters and figures in the same number is
fanciful....  This is the best plan I can conceive for alfabetical
arrangement and I hope some one will make the necessary table for
applying it.  I have heretofore rather opposed all translating
systems because I had not tried them or studied them thoroughly
enough to appreciate their merits.  If alfabetical arrangement is
to be secured at all I am now converted to this plan, and trust
no one else will have to give as much time and labor to its study.[9]
```

7. Melvil Dewey, "Plans for numbering, with especial reference to fiction : a library symposium," *Library journal* 4 (February 1879): 42–44.

8. Charles Ammi Cutter, "Plans for numbering, with especial reference to fiction : a library symposium," *Library journal* 4 (February 1879): 44–46.

9. Dewey, "Plans for numbering, with especial reference to fiction," p. 47.

In another article of the issue of *Library journal* which contained the symposium on book numbers, John Edmands tabulated the results of his analyses of five library author catalogs and of one biographical dictionary and compared the results of these analyses with one done by Jacob Schwartz earlier.[10] These analyses were done to determine the correct proportions of names which begin with the same initial letter. Two years later in 1881 A. P. Massey analyzed several biographical dictionaries in order to discover the necessary quantity of numbers which would be necessary for each letter of the alphabet to make an author number table with appropriate distributions of numbers.[11] Schwartz, Edmands, and Massey had carefully analyzed the problem of the distribution of numbers for author tables before the publication of any Cutter author number table. (These analyses and others are discussed in full detail in the following chapter.)

It did not take Cutter very long to realize that Edmands's idea was probably the best, because just four months later he was using decimal numbers preceded by the initial letter of the author's surname. During May and June 1879 Cutter directed the compilation of a book catalog for the public library of Winchester, Massachusetts.[12] The books listed in this catalog are classified by Cutter's own classification scheme, sometimes called the "Boston Athenaeum classification," which was the forerunner of his *Expansive classification*. The novels are arranged alphabetically by author and assigned an author number consisting of the initial letter of the author's surname and followed by decimal numbers representing the remaining letters. Thus Cutter was already experimenting with the idea of using the initial letter and following it with numbers as John Edmands had suggested. However, none of the author numbers used in this catalog corresponds to any which were published in his two-figure table a few years later. These numbers also vary from those of Cutter's two-figure and three-figure tables in that the vowels and the letter S only use the initial letter instead of two or three letters as Cutter advocated with later editions. The following entries are examples taken from the Winchester catalog:

Abbott.	Rollo in London.	A025 RL
Abbott.	Rollo in Naples.	A025 RN
Alcott.	My girls, etc.	A31 MG
Aldrich.	Queen of Sheeba.	A32 Q

10. John Edmands, "Proportion of initial letters in author catalogs," *Library journal* 4 (February 1879): 56.

11. A. P. Massey, "Classification of fiction," *Library journal* 6 (January 1881):7–9.

12. Winchester Town Library, *Class- and author-lists* ([Winchester, Mass.: The Library], 1879).

Alger.	Paul the peddler.	A343 P
Arthur.	Nothing but money.	A79 N
Austen.	Pride and prejudice.	A933 P
Cary.	Picture of country life.	C16
Charles.	Lapsed but not lost.	C30 L
Collins.	Poor Miss Finch.	C64 P
Cupples.	Green hand.	C90
Savage.	Bluffton.	S102
Scott.	Red gauntlet.	S31 R
Shepherd.	Faith and Patience.	S4274
Shillaber.	Ike Partington.	S43
Smith.	Jolly good times.	S605 J
Stowe.	Minister's wooing.	S85 M
Stretton.	Queen of the county.	S865 Q

In 1880 Cutter printed a preliminary version if his two-figure table. The following brief notice appeared in *Library journal*:

> Boston.--Mr. Cutter has printed his table for keeping authors alfabetically arranged on the shelf, by a combination of numbers following the initial letters of the authors' names. Copies are for sale.[13]

Thus the first of the Cutter tables was begun. Even though there are no known extant copies of this first printed Cutter table it is known that there were some changes made during the years between the printing of this preliminary version and the publication of the two-figure table a few years later. Cutter used this early version in the classification of books at the Boston Athenaeum. In 1882 he published a guide for the users of the Boston Athenaeum in which he explained his classification scheme and the new system of "author-marks." The explanation is very clear and concise, and he used many examples to illustrate the classification numbers and the "author-marks." About 16 percent of the "author-marks" do not correspond to those

---

13. *Library journal* 5 (September-October 1880): 293.

in his two-figure table, published a few years later. Thus it is known that he was still experimenting and working on a final version of his *Alfabetic-order table*, but that by 1882 it was almost in its final form. About these "author-marks" Cutter wrote:

This author-mark is composed of the initial of the author's family name followed by figures assigned according to a table which is so constructed that the names in which G is followed by one of the <u>first</u> letters in the alphabet have the <u>first</u> numbers and those in which it is followed by <u>later</u> letters have <u>later</u> numbers, <u>e.g.</u>

Gardiner,	G16	Gerry,	G36
Gilman,	G42	Glover,	G51
Gore,	G66	Graham,	G76
Grote,	G89	Guizot,	G94

If the books are arranged in the order of these numbers of course they will be in alphabetical order.

The table is made in this way: All the names in G, from Gaa to Gyz, are divided into nine parts. Any one falling within the second [i.e., first] part (which runs from G to Garo) is numbered G1, any one falling within the second part (Gas to Geo) is numbered G2, and so on. As there may often be several names falling within each part, provision is made to distinguish them by adding another figure. Just as the whole of the names beginning with G are divided into nine parts, so the names in the first part (G to Garo) are again subdivided into nine parts, the first (G to Gae) numbered 1, the second (Gaf to Gak) numbered 2, and so on.

This gives us the following table:--

Names beginning with any combination between

G and Gas, inclusive, are numbered G11

Names beginning with any combination between

```
    Gaf and Gak, inclusive, are numbered . . . . . . . . .   G12

Names beginning with Gal are numbered . . . . . . . . . .   G13

    "         "       "  Gam  "        "   . . . . . . . . . . .   G14

Names beginning with any combination between

    Gan and Gaq, inclusive, are numbered . . . . . . . .   G15

And so on.

    Then in the second part of G (Gas to Geo):--

Names beginning with Gas are numbered . . . . . . . . . .   G21

    "         "       "  Gat  "        "   . . . . . . . . . . .   G22

    "         "       "  Gau  "        "   . . . . . . . . . . .   G23

And so on.

    If there are several names beginning with Gas, then G21 is

likewise divided into nine parts, G211, G212, G213, G214, etc.

And if several names still fall within the limits covered by

G211, that would be farther divided into G2111, G2112, G2113,

etc.  So that however many names there may be, it will always

be possible to give each a number that will distinguish it from

every name, and will keep it in its place in the alphabet.[14]
```

Melvil Dewey was a great promoter of his convictions, and his ideas and opinions were very influential in this period of development of librarianship. Dewey was fully convinced that the use of author numbers was the best system for subarranging books under the same classification number. Dewey was using Cutter's author table in conjunction with his own *Decimal classification* as early as 1882. A notice in *Library journal* about the recataloging and reclassification of the library of Wellesley College stated:

```
    After investigation of the various methods, the Dui [i.e.,

Dewey] system has been adopted, and reclassification and recatalog-

ing is going forward under the direction of the Library Bureau. . . .

For book numbers he [Melvil Dewey] has adopted as best the Cutter
```

14. Cutter, *How to get books, with an explanation of the new way of marking books*, pp. 14–15.

system of initials of authors' names, followed by numbers repre-

senting the rest of the name.[15]

On August 14, 1883, at the Buffalo Conference of the American Library Association during a discussion of "close classification" Dewey made the following comments:

> The author arrangement <u>under close classification</u>, so far from
>
> being "old fogy," is the latest fashion. For the past five years
>
> I have noted its growing use, and always with satisfaction to the
>
> users. Since the plans of translating names into numbers, devised
>
> by Messrs. Schwartz, Cutter, and Edmands, came into use most of
>
> the difficulties of this plan are met, and it is now the growing
>
> method. While for the final arrangement after the books have
>
> been distributed into classes, divisions, sections, this seems
>
> best, care must be taken not to confuse this "alphabetical plan"
>
> with that used at the N.Y. State and N.Y. Mercantile libraries.
>
> Their plan puts all the Smiths, for example, that have written
>
> on all conceivable subjects, into one dreadful row from which to
>
> hunt out the Smith you want. It has all the disadvantages, great
>
> or small, of the relative location, and very few of its advantages.
>
> To my mind, after special study of shelf-arrangement for ten years,
>
> the alphabetical plan under the final subject classes is the best,
>
> and the same plan for the whole library, without subject classing,
>
> is the worst with which I am acquainted.[16]

Other librarians were also assigning author numbers from Cutter's table and appear to have been greatly pleased with the results. In a letter dated February 2, 1885, the Rev. Mr. E. N. Goddard of Windsor, Vermont, wrote that he had just finished classifying his fiction collection using the *Decimal*

---

15. "Dui's doings," *Library journal* 7 (September 1882): 237.
16. Melvil Dewey, [Comments in the] "Proceedings of the Buffalo Conference," *Library journal* 8 (September-October, 1883): 275.

classification and the "Cutter author-numbers." About the use of the table he commented:

> It is already evident that the change will be an improvement, and we shall, as leisure allows, extend it to other sections of the library--probably to the biography class (920) next.[17]

The following year another letter appeared in *Library journal* which not only commended Cutter for his author table, but also brought up a very important point about the distribution of the numbers among the twenty-six letters. Charles H. Swan wrote:

> I find the [Cutter author] table very useful for its legitimate purpose--for bringing the book numbers in harmony with an arrangement by authors' names in advance of the final development of a library. I am also using it for another purpose. . . . I am arranging my reports, pamphlets, etc., by names of places as an expansion of the subject number, using the alfabet.-order table to translate : e.g., all reports on Boston Sewerage stand under 627, 209 B65. . . .
>
> So far as I have used the table in this way it has worked well, but it seems to me that the principle needed in a universal alfab.-order table for names of places may require a different law of averages from that governing authors' names.[18]

The Cutter author table was not only being used by librarians to assign cutter numbers and subarrange materials under the same classification number, but it also stirred the imaginations of librarians to find other uses for this idea of initial letters followed by digits to arrange items in an orderly fashion. In 1885 Walter Stanley Biscoe (1853–1933), cataloger at Columbia College, devised a table for the chronological subarrangement of materials using a symbol similar to a cutter author number in which a letter is followed by digits. Like most other libraries of that period the one at Columbia College

---

17. E. N. Goddard, "Classification of fiction," *Library journal* 10 (March 1885): 55.
18. Charles H. Swan, "Alfab.-order table for names of places," *Library journal* 11 (April 1886): 118.

previously had assigned a fixed place on a fixed shelf for each book. Biscoe credited Cutter, Edmands, and Schwartz for the basic idea of his time table used in subarranging books chronologically under each classification number. Science was selected as the subject area for the experiment with the time table at Columbia. Science was chosen because Biscoe believed that the science books most frequently used were those most recently published, and that it would be more logical and practical to give them a chronological arrangement rather than one by author. Book numbers representing the year of publication or copyright were formed from the following table:

A.	B.C.	F.	1700–1799	K.	1840–1849
B.	A.D.–999	G.	1800–1809	L.	1850–1859
C.	1000–1499	H.	1810–1819	M.	1860–1869
D.	1500–1599	I.	1820–1829	N.	1870–1879
E.	1600–1699	J.	1830–1839	O.	1880–1889

The letters A and B were followed by the year in which the books had been written. The letter C was followed by the last three digits of the year, thus a book written in 1340 was assigned the book number C340, one written in 1472 was assigned C472. For the years 1500 to 1799 only two digits were used, for example, for the year 1520 the book number was D20, for 1672 it was E72, and 1778 was F78. Each decade of the nineteenth century only required one letter and one digit; therefore, a book written in 1815 was assigned H5, one from 1848 was K8, and 1852 was L2. Biscoe urged a very minute classification to reduce the quantity of books under each classification number. However, Biscoe made no mention of how to distinguish between two books written on the same subject and published in the same year, but logically they would first be arranged by subject, then by year, and lastly by author. Biscoe was not concerned that his table would reach its limit with the letter Z in the year 1999, and commented that before this limit was reached someone would have devised a better scheme.[19]

A few years later in 1893 another librarian, C. R. Olin of Buchtel College (later the University of Akron), created a table to be used for collective biographies. This was also based on Cutter's plan and was designed for use in conjunction with Cutter's two-figure table in which all names beginning with vowels used the first two letters followed by a single digit. Olin's idea was to arrange all collective biographies preceding the individual ones. He used the letter A followed by the numbers 11 to 99 to represent all names from A to Z of compilers and editors of collective biographies, for example, Adams was assigned the number A11, Baker was A12, Lane A52, Young A98, and Zeller A99. Olin pointed out that the single letter A followed by digits would

19. Walter Stanley Biscoe, "Chronological arrangement on shelves," *Library journal* 10 (September-October 1885): 246–47.

precede all book numbers beginning with the letter followed by another letter and digits. Thus all collective biographies would be arranged alphabetically by the editor or compiler and would precede the individual biographies arranged alphabetically by biographee.[20]

The following examples illustrate the implementation of Olin's plan.

A12	Barnhart. New century cyclopedia of names.
A17	Chambers's biographical dictionary.
A44	Hyamson. A dictionary of universal biography of all ages and of all peoples.
A45	International who's who.
A87	Thomas. Universal pronouncing dictionary of biography and mythology.
A94	Webster's biographical dictionary.
Ab2	Biography of Jacob Abbott.
Ac8	Acton : the formative years.
Ad1	Robert Adam in his circle in Edinburgh and Rome.
Ae8	Aeschylus : the creation of tragedy.
An2	Life and times of Hans Christian Anderson.
B45	Berlioz and the romantic century.
H36	Heinrich Heine : the artist in revolt.
Ib7	Ibsen the master builder.
Or9	Orwell : a literary and biographical study.
Z7	Zoffany and his Tribuna.

Olin's table could not be used with Sanborn's revision of Cutter's author table in which all names beginning with vowels used only the initial letter followed by digits, because there would be no distinguishing factor between the collective biographies and the individual ones.

Melvil Dewey so esteemed Cutter's author number plan and Biscoe's time table that he mentioned them in his introduction to the second edition (1885)

---

20. C. R. Olin, "An order table for collective biography," *Library journal* 18 (May 1893): 144.

of the *Decimal classification*. In this introduction Dewey explained three different ideas for subarranging books under the same classification number by saying:

> Accompanying the class number is the <u>book</u> number, which prevents confusion of different books on the same subject. Thus the first Geometry cataloged is marked 513.1; the second, 513.2, and so on to any extent, the last number showing how many books the library has on that subject. . . .
>
> Since the invention of the translation systems by which the author's name is represented by its initial with the rest of the name translated into numbers (e. g. Freeman would be F 87,) most libraries prefer to arrange the books under each class number alfabetically by authors. This keeps all the works by the same author together, and in large classes enables one to find any book redily without consulting the catalog.
>
> A third arrangement of the books under class numbers is chronologically by dates of first publication. Its advantage is in presenting the historical development of the subject, the book written earliest being on the left, the latest work on the right, and then of any given book it is evident that all those on the left were written before it, all those on the right after it. In science this has special value, while in litera-ture the author arrangement is better. A translation system of dates makes the numbering of the year more compact and satis-factory.[21]

A year later in 1886 Dewey presented some basic ideas on book numbers at the Milwaukee Conference of the American Library Association. This is undoubtedly the most complete and analytical discussion of the various

21. Melvil Dewey, *Decimal classification and relativ index*, 2d ed. (Boston: Library Bureau, 1885), pp 35, 37.

methods of subarranging books that has ever appeared in the literature. The following are summaries of Dewey's twelve points of discussion:

1. The subject of book numbers is very important because it has much to do with rapid, accurate, and economical administration.
2. The question of book numbers is entirely distinct from classification and it applies no more to the Decimal Classification than to any other.
3. All libraries are now classifying at least broadly, and a growing number are using a close classification.
4. Since libraries are classifying their collections this means that the books are in a relative location rather than a fixed location that so many libraries used previously.
5. Book numbers should be simple, brief, and useful. The quality given the greatest emphasis depends on the type of library, its clientele, and the competencies of its staff.
6. There are only two systems of symbols that have a fixed order well enough known to be used for marking books, viz., Arabic numerals and the Roman alphabet. The use of any other characters would only cause confusion.
7. The simplest way to subarrange books under each classification number is a numerical arrangement, 1, 2, 3, etc. But, this has two great disadvantages: (1) the author, date, publisher, language, style of treatment are entirely disregarded and only an accession order exists, and (2) there is no way to locate a specific book except to know its precise number, while Cutter numbers arrange them by authors.
8. A subarrangement by authors under the classification number facilitates its location without consulting the catalog. When book numbers are used instead of the names of the authors it takes less time to arrange the shelves, locate a particular item, and charge it out to the borrower.
9. The subarrangement of books by the year of publication can be useful in the areas of science and the useful arts and presents an order otherwise unavailable. Only libraries with open stacks should adopt it because in a library with closed stacks there is no advantage whatsoever.
10. There are only three methods that are really being used, viz., (1) the numerical, i.e., 1, 2, 3, etc., (2) authors, and (3) the time plan, i.e., by year of publication. Other methods which have been suggested but are considered to be "bad methods" are arrangements by publisher, color, cost, style of treatment, merit, title, language, and by further subject division.

11. Eclectic book numbers seem to be simplest. These are letters that follow the classification number, i.e., an arrangement from a to z. The letter can be the author's initial and when necessary the decimal principle can be applied, i.e., between c and d, c5 can be intercalated; between c and c5, c3 can be easily inserted.
12. The arrangement of books by size is often used in private libraries, but this is "utter nonsense."

Dewey ended these *ex cathedra* remarks by saying that if he had failed to make his points that he would be glad to hear from any critic or inquirer.[22]

There was no introductory section in the third (1888) edition of the *Decimal classification*, but in the fourth, fifth, and sixth editions (1891, 1894, and 1899) Dewey advocated the use of the Biscoe time table as well as the Cutter table by writing:

BOOK NUMBERS

Author numbers.--The invention of translation systems by which a name is represented by its initial with the rest translated into numbers,--e.g., Freeman, F 87,--has led most libraries to arrange books under each class number alfabetically by authors, or in local history by towns, or in biografy by biografees. This keeps all works by the same author together, and in large classes enables one to find any book readily without consulting catalogs. One great advantage is that the same author has the same book number in every subject; i.e., the figures are significant like our class numbers, and translate themselves into the name. Great practical mnemonic convenience results from this peculiar form of book number. By far the most widely used of these translation systems is that of the Boston Athenaeum, devised by the librarian, C. A. Cutter, and known as the Cutter numbers.

22. Melvil Dewey, "Eclectic book-numbers," *Library journal* 11 (August-September 1886): 296–301.

Time numbers.--A second arrangement of books under class numbers
is chronological by dates of first publication. Its advantage is in
presenting the historical development of the subject, the book
written earliest being on the left, the latest work on the right,
and then of any given book it is evident that all those on the left
were written before it, all those on the right after it. In science
this has special value, while in literature the author arrangement is
better. A translation system of dates devised by W. S. Biscoe, makes
the numbering of the year more compact and satisfactory than to write
the date in full.[23]

Dewey's recommendation that the Cutter book numbers be used with his *Decimal classification* certainly influenced their success. Dewey's recommendation of the Biscoe time numbers may have been influenced by his long and strong relationship with Biscoe. In his "Aknowlejments" that appeared in the eleventh, twelfth, thirteenth, and fourteenth editions (1922, 1927, 1932, and 1942) of his *Decimal classification*, Dewey included the following paragraph about Biscoe:

From 1st publication to the present, the most extended and
valued assistance has cum from my colej clasmate, associate and
frend, Walter Stanley Biscoe, my 1st assistant in Amherst College
Library, in charj of which he succeeded me, resyning to accept
again in 1883 the place next me in Columbia College Library, and
again resyning in 1889 to becum librarian in charj of clasification
and catalogs in New York State Library. This book is witness to the

23. Melvil Dewey, *Decimal classification and relativ index*, 4th ed. (Boston: Library Bureau, 1891), p. 30.
_____. _____. 5th ed. (Boston: Library Bureau, 1894), p. 30.
_____. _____. 6th ed. (Boston: Library Bureau, 1899), p. 30.

```
rare unselfishness with which he has givn time taken from rest and

recreation to this work, in which he shared my interest and faith.²⁴
```

There is no doubt about Dewey's conviction concerning the usefulness of the Biscoe time table and the Olin collective biography table in library classification; otherwise he would not have included the complete Biscoe and Olin tables at the end of editions seven through thirteen (1911-1932) of his *Decimal classification.*²⁵

Cutter is also the first person to have used author numbers to bring about an orderly and logical subarrangement of works by and about a particular author. In 1884 he presented an arrangement for Shakespeare.²⁶ In his "Boston Athenaeum classification" English literature was represented by "VE" and he used author numbers to subarrange the books by and about Shakespeare. A synopsis of this subarrangement is:

```
          S1 - S5  Shakspere's works

S1, S2  Editions of the Works, arranged chronologically.

S3      Translations, arranged by languages and then by translators.

S4      Selections, Imitations, Tales founded on the plays.

S5      Separate plays and poems, with their translations.
```

24. Melvil Dewey, *Decimal classification and relativ index*, 11th ed. (Lake Placid Club, N.Y.: Forest Press, 1922), p. 43.
———. ———. 12th ed. (Lake Placid Club, N.Y.: Forest Press, 1927), p. 47.
———. ———. 13th ed. (Lake Placid Club, N.Y.: Forest Press, 1932), p. 47.
———. ———. 14th ed. (Lake Placid Club, N.Y.: Forest Press, 1942), p. 47.
25. Melvil Dewey, *Decimal classification and relativ index*, 7th ed. (Lake Placid Club, N.Y.: Forest Press, 1911), pp. [789–91].
———. ———. 8th ed. (Lake Placid Club, N.Y.: Forest Press, 1913), pp. [806–8].
———. ———. 9th ed. (Lake Placid Club, N.Y.: Forest Press, 1915), pp. 854–56.
———. ———. 10th ed. (Lake Placid Club, N.Y.: Forest Press, 1919), pp. 934–36.
———. ———. 11th ed. (Lake Placid Club, N.Y.: Forest Press, 1922), pp. 984–86.
———. ———. 12th ed. (Lake Placid Club, N.Y.: Forest Press, 1927), pp. 1239–41.
———. ———. 13th ed. (Lake Placid Club, N.Y.: Forest Press, 1932), pp. 1643–45.
Note: The Introduction to the 14th edition (1942) contained the following statement on page 33: "For ful explanations see 'Biscoe time numbers,' on pajes following Relativ index." But, for some reason the Biscoe time table and the Olin collective biography table were not included as stated, and have not been included in any successive edition.
26. Charles Ammi Cutter, "Arrangement and notation for Shaksperiana," *Library journal* 9 (August 1884): 137–39.

```
                    S6 - S9   Shaksperiana

             (S6-S8 about the Works; S9 about the man.)

    S6       General and miscellaneous works, incl. periodicals and

             publications of societies.

    S7       Criticism and commentaries.

    S8       Bibliografy and literary history.

    S9       Biografy.
```

Two years later Cutter published a special table for Latin and Greek authors in which a subarrangement for works by and about a particular author was presented.[27] This subarrangement has a more universal application than the one he prepared for Shakespeare. From his remarks about the Biscoe time numbers it is obvious that Cutter did not like them as well as Dewey did. Some of his comments about the subarrangement of an author's works and the Biscoe time numbers are:

> I have prepared a table of equivalents for or transliterations
> [i.e., changing letters of a name to numbers] of the names of Greek
> and Latin authors, so devised that with few characters one can give
> a separate mark to every author, to every one of his works, and to
> every edition of each work, and that these marks should keep the
> authors alfabetically arranged, and their works alfabetically
> subarranged, and the editions in chronological order.
>
> The great difficulty in the use of transliteration tables is
> that one can never foresee who will write books, and after one has
> used the best judgment in guessing the future one may find oneself
> compelled to intercalate an unexpected name in some place where
> intercalation means long numbers. But there is no such drawback to
> their use for the classics. One knows just how many names one has
> to provide for; the roll is made up; one can use a minimum of figures

27. Charles Ammi Cutter, "Author-tables for Greek and Latin authors," *Library journal* 11 (August-September 1886): 280–89.

in assigning them symbols, without fear that any new-comer will disturb the order.

The order adopted is: 1, whole works, chronologically arranged; 2, translations of whole works alfabetically arranged by the languages; 3, dictionaries, commentaries, and other illustrative works; 4, selections; 5, single works, each with the same three divisions that the whole works have.

The method of marking may be shown by an example: Paley's frogs would be marked V for Literature; P for Greek, A7 for Aristophanes, R for Ranae, 1878 because published in that year, or all together VP·A7R 1878. Rogers's translation of the Lysistrata would be L. for Lysistrata, E for English, and R for Rogers,--thus: VP·A7L.ER.

It will be noticed that the year is written in full. Mr. Biscoe's scheme for giving dates briefly is admirable. It has only two defects. First, it is not self-interpreting; it does not suggest its meaning, but has to be understood by a sheer effort of memory. But I do not see how this could be otherwise; if I did I would make a better table. Secondly, it will not last long enough; it stops at A.D. 2000. I suppose this seems a long way ahead to our younger members, who do not know how time flies. Let them "wait till" they "come to forty year." 2000 A.D. will be here before they know it. Nevertheless, I use the table in one section of the Athenaeum and mean to use it elsewhere. But in the classics it seemed better to put on the backs of the books a mark which everybody could understand at a glance,-- the usual date, 1886, 1494, etc. With our system of charging the four figures cause no delay, and the greater clumsiness of the mark when used as a call-number is compensated by its greater intelligibility on the shelf.[28]

28. Ibid., p. 280.

The following examples are from this special table for Greek and Latin authors.[29]

Latin Authors		Greek Authors	
Catullus	C5	Aeschylus	A2
Celsus	C6	Aesopus	A3
Charisius	C68	Aristophanes	A7
Petronius	P3	Empedocles	E2
Phaedrus	P4	Emphorus	E25
Phocas	P43	Epicurus	E3
Plautus	P5	Eupolemus	E78

Cutter's first edition of the *Alfabetic-order table* was published sometime around 1886.[30] This edition differed from the earlier preliminary version printed in 1880 in that some of the numbers from this edition do not correspond to examples given in Cutter's guide of 1882, *How to get books, with an explanation of the new way of marking books*.[31] Examples:

1882			1886
G36		Gerry	G32
G89		Grote	G91

Even though many libraries had been using cutter numbers for several years it was not until 1887 that Cutter published instructions on the use of the *Alfabetic-order table*. These instructions appeared in an article entitled "How to use Cutter's decimal author table," which was more of a list of general principles on book numbers rather than instructions on the use of the table itself.[32]

---

29. Ibid., pp. 281–85.

30. An exact date of publication could not be determined from any source. There can be little doubt that the table was first published either in 1886 or 1887. Library catalogs give dates ranging from 1885 to 1887. Cutter published the first instructions on the use of the table in *Library journal* in July 1887. Therefore it is most probable that the table was published a few months earlier. This would fix the date as sometime at the end of 1886 or early in 1887. The year 1886 is given here as this seems to be the most plausible.

31. Cutter, *How to get books, with an explanation of the new way of marking books*, p. 14.

32. Charles Ammi Cutter, "How to use Cutter's decimal author table," *Library journal* 12 (July 1887): 251–52 and (December 1887): 549.

Early in 1888 Cutter revised and reprinted his two-figure table. He expanded the 1886 edition from 2,576 numbers for the twenty-six letters to 2,727. The following changes were made: A was increased just one number, from 233 to 234; E was expanded from 164 numbers to 234; I increased from 161 numbers to 198; O increased from 215 to 225; S expanded from 255 to 297 numbers; and the letter Z was decreased from 18 to 9 numbers. In an announcement published in *Library journal*, of the revised *Alfabetic-order table* Cutter explained that the table had been reprinted in larger type with the correction of a few typographical errors. He continued by saying that the positions of some of the letters had been changed and that some letters had been expanded so that all groups would be in regular sets of nine to facilitate use of the table. It was also pointed out that in this new table the letters with 11 to 99 tables would appear on the left side and that the letters with 1 to 9 tables would be printed on the right side, because in the first edition the letter W, an 11 to 99 letter, was on the right side among the 1 to 9 tables and this had led some persons to use it with a vowel. Cutter offered this revised table free to those who had bought the first edition.[33]

That same year (1888) at the Annual Conference of the American Library Association held in the Catskills of upstate New York, there was a symposium on Tuesday, September 25, entitled, "Cutter author-numbers in connection with the Dewey Classification." The participants were:

A. N. Brown, librarian, U.S. Naval Academy, Annapolis, Maryland

Mary Salome Cutler (1855-1921), instructor, Columbia College Library School, New York City

Charles A. Cutter (1837-1903), librarian, Boston Athenaeum, Boston, Massachusetts

Herbert E. Davidson, Library Bureau, Boston, Massachusetts

William I. Fletcher (1844-1917), librarian, Amherst College, Amherst, Massachusetts

Gardner Maynard Jones (1850-1941), student, Columbia College Library School, New York City

Josephus Nelson Larned (1836-1913), librarian, Buffalo Library, Buffalo, New York

Charles C. Soule, trustee, Brookline Public Library, Brookline, Massachusetts.

The symposium as it was recorded in the conference issue of *Library journal* reads:

---

33. Charles Ammi Cutter, "Cutter, C: A. Alfabetic-order table," *Library journal* 13, (March-April 1888): 107.

CUTTER AUTHOR-NUMBERS IN CONNECTION WITH

THE DEWEY CLASSIFICATION

Have any present used this combination?

<u>Mr. Davidson</u>.--I should say that at least twenty libraries
are using it.

<u>Mr. Brown</u>.--Will Mr. Fletcher tell us what is in use at Amherst?

<u>Mr. Fletcher</u>.--What Mr. Dewey might call a crude application of
his system. The attempt was made to use separate shelves for 4°s,
8°s, and 12°s. The librarian at Bangor reports no difficulty in using
the long combination of numbers given in their new catalog.

<u>Mr. Jones</u>.--Columbia College Library does not use the Cutter
author-numbers in all classes. Mr. Biscoe's time-numbers are used
in books arranged chronologically. In Fiction for brevity the call-
number is omitted and author-numbers only are used.

<u>Mr. Cutter</u>.--In the Winchester Library I suggested the use of a
V check instead of the class mark for Fiction.

<u>Miss M. S. Cutler</u>.--In some small libraries the class-number for
Fiction is ignored, and the author-number only is used.

<u>Mr. Soule</u>.--Is there any other subject, so large as Fiction,
where class and author-numbers can be combined?

<u>Mr. Cutter</u>.--Biography.

<u>Mr. Fletcher</u>.--Do you use the author-numbers in all classes?

<u>Mr. Cutter</u>.--Yes, even in classes where we use Biscoe time-
numbers, for we put the latter into the class-number.

<u>Mr. Soule</u>.--I should think the long call-numbers of the Bangor
Library would make confusion, and errors be made by the uninstructed
public.

Pres. Cutter read a letter from Mary H. Curran, Asst. Librarian
at Bangor, Me., reporting: "We have used the Dewey classification in

full with the addition of the Cutter author symbols, and have been perfectly satisfied with the result."

Mr. Fletcher.--I think the combination of letters and figures leads to trouble.

Mr. Cutter.--I think the combination of letters and numbers leads to just the opposite result. The mind does not easily grasp mor~ than 4 or 5 letters or figures. That is the reason why in numerals we mark each group of three by a comma (3,461,229). In the same way letters interposed throw class marks into groups that are easily taken in by the eye. B29F44 is more easily read than BVDGMO or 129744.

Mr. Fletcher.--A lady of Winchester recently told me she could make neither head nor tail of the Winchester method.

Mr. Cutter.--A lady this summer asked me if I did not think the Winchester combination of letters and numbers the worst possible. [Laughter.] I was much taken aback, as it was the first intimation I had had that it was not liked, for the librarian always reports that there is no trouble.

I want to ask Miss Cutler if good comes in all classes from the alphabetical arrangement?

Miss Cutler.--We do not use the author-numbers in all classes at Columbia; time-numbers are used in Science and Useful arts, the Cutter numbers in History, Sociology, Philology, and Literature. In Philosophy, Religion, and Fine arts a simple initial of the author's name is used, followed by a number in accession order; these are smaller classes, less used, and so there is a saving in length of call-number. In larger classes there would be little saving.

Mr. Larned.--How much do you use the time numbers, Mr. Cutter?

```
Mr. Cutter.--I find some use for them, but the alphabetical

arrangement in all classes in my library is of constant use.[34]
```

The ideas and opinions expressed by the participants of this symposium strongly demonstrate the popularity of Cutter's author numbers as well as the fact that they were being widely used by libraries which classified their collections with Dewey's *Decimal classification*.

Summary

The basic element in book numbers is the translation or conversion of letters into numbers, which when arranged numerically will also be an alphabetical order of the names represented by the numbers. The prototype was devised by Jacob Schwartz. Cutter liked Schwartz's idea better than Dewey's method of simply adding a number as part of the call number which only showed the order in which the books with the same classification number were cataloged and classified in a particular library. John Edmands added another facet to book numbers by suggesting that the initial letter of the author's surname precede the digits. Cutter improved on this by using numbers which were to be treated as decimals rather than as integers, thus allowing for infinite intercalation of new book numbers without disturbing the alphabetical order. Cutter was also the first person to publish a table which would serve as a guide for converting names into numbers and sell it to libraries for this purpose. Librarians enthusiastically accepted the idea of subarranging books by author under each classification number and by the end of the 1880s the assigning of "Cutter numbers" had become a standard procedure in library classification.

34. "Cutter author-numbers in connection with the Dewey Classification," *Library journal* 13 (September-October 1888): 308–9.

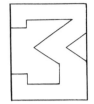

Development
of the Cutter Tables

By 1890 it was common practice in many libraries to assign "cutter numbers" to all classified books. However, many libraries were finding the two-figure table inadequate for their collections and Cutter decided to expand the table to three digits. He made arrangements with Kate Emery Sanborn in 1892 to undertake the work of expanding the table. Sanborn had worked as a cataloger under Cutter's direction at the Boston Athenaeum from 1883 to 1891 and had resigned her position in Boston to become cataloger at the Mercantile Library of St. Louis. She worked in St. Louis from February 1, 1891, until March 1894, when she accepted the position of librarian of the Manchester (N.H.) Public Library. She remained there until her marriage to Gardner Maynard Jones, librarian of the Salem (Mass.) Public Library, on June 30, 1897. After her marriage she used the name Kate Emery Jones, and it is under this name that she appears in indexes and biographical dictionaries.

It was during those years away from Massachusetts and from Cutter that Sanborn prepared the two tables that were later to be more popular than Cutter's own work. The first of these tables consisted only of the vowels and the letter S. In this table she expanded the numbers for the letters A and S to three digits, and the letters E, I, O, and U to two digits. Many librarians had found that two digits were insufficient for A and S. This was meant to be just an alternative table to be used in conjunction with Cutter's two-figure table, but Sanborn did not follow the original table when she expanded these six letters. A notice appearing in the November 1892 issue of *Library journal* stated that Cutter had found many persons disliked his use of two or three letters for the vowels and the letter S and preferred just one letter followed by digits, as had been done for the other letters of the alphabet. For this reason he had asked Kate E. Sanborn to prepare a table where the vowels and the letter S would be treated like the consonants of his original table. Sanborn also used three figures for the letters A and S, but found that three figures were not necessary for the vowels E, I, O, and U. Sanborn's table was published in 1892 and sold by Cutter for one dollar.[1]

During the short time that Kate Sanborn was in St. Louis she prepared a catalog, also published in 1892, of the English prose fiction in the Mercantile Library.[2] All the fiction listed in this catalog was classified under the number 7 and followed by an author number from Cutter's two-figure table. Some examples from this catalog are:

```
About, Edmond F. V. Germaine
       King of the mountains.          7.Ab7k
       Notary's nose.                  7.Ab7no

Lyall, Edna
       Hardy norseman.                 7.L98h
       In the golden days.             7.L98i

Scott, Sir Walter
       Monastery.                      7.Sco85m
       Peveril of the peak.            7.Sco85p
       Pirate.                         7.Sco85pi
```

Sanborn probably did not use her new table for the vowels and the letter S in this catalog because she had not yet completed her table of consonants and felt that the author numbers should be uniform throughout. There is little doubt that Sanborn had already arrived at the conclusion that it would be simpler and more practical to consistently use just the initial letter and two or three digits for all letters of the alphabet, rather than Cutter's system of using two letters for the vowels and the letter S, and three letters for names beginning with the letters Sc. Cutter even continued to advocate the use of two or three letters for the vowels and the letter S with his three-figure table published in 1901.[3]

In 1895 Sanborn finished a table for the other twenty letters of the alphabet (the consonants, except S). This table was published by Library Bureau and announced in the October issue of *Library journal.*[4]

1. *Library journal* 17 (November 1892): 468.
2. St. Louis Mercantile Library, *Catalogue of the St. Louis Mercantile Library, section 1, English prose fiction* (St. Louis: Nixon-Jones Printing Co., 1892).
3. Charles Ammi Cutter, *Explanation of the alphabetic-order marks (three-figure tables)* (Northampton, Mass.: C. A. Pierce & Company, 1901), p. 4.
4. *Library journal* 20 (October 1895): 363.

The two tables of Sanborn, (1) vowels and the letter S, and (2) consonants, except S, were combined and printed in a single table a year or so later.

Because Sanborn was so far away from Cutter during her work on the three-figure table, he had been unable to supervise her in this task. She made a three-figure table completely independent of Cutter's two-figure table, and only very few numbers corresponded to the original table. Sanborn's table for the vowels and consonants is based on her idea that it would be better to use only the initial letter for all names regardless of the fact that they begin with a vowel or a consonant. Cutter had intended this new table to be only an expansion, with all numbers in the new table corresponding to those in the original table. Libraries that had used the two-figure table encountered many conflicts in the author numbers assigned from the two different tables. Cutter was quite disturbed by this and decided to make a new three-figure table for use by those libraries which already had collections with numbers assigned from the two-figure table. The August 1899 issue of *Library journal* contained an announcement that Cutter had begun work on an expansion of his original table. He also mentioned that the "new tables will be printed on manila paper, which will make them much pleasanter to use than the heavy boards on which the Cutter-Sanborn tables were mounted. They will not last as long, but they can be sold at a less price."[5]

Five months after Cutter's announcement, he commented in a letter to *Public libraries* that he would entrust this task to "two friends." It is not known who these two friends were; also in this letter Kate Sanborn is referred to only as a "volunteer." The brief article concerning the new table reads as follows:

Some discussion has been going on lately among librarians in some of the smaller libraries in the West anent the relation which exists between the two-figure and the three-figure order tables. The subject having been brought to Mr. Cutter's attention, he writes of it as follows:

I intended the three-figure order tables to be an extension of the two-figure tables; but through some misunderstanding the new ones were made without any reference to their predecessors, so that the two cannot be used together. I could not ask a volunteer to do her work over again, and so I printed them.

5. *Library journal* 24 (August 1899), 501.

```
Experience has shown that this was a mistake; therefore, I have

entrusted to two friends the preparation of new three-figure

tables, made as I intended the other to be, by adding a third

figure to my two.  As soon as they are done I shall print them.⁶
```

The new table was completed in 1901 and was announced for sale in January 1902. From the notices that Cutter placed in *Library journal* and in *Public libraries* it appears that he was trying to make sure that libraries would use his new three-figure table and abandon the one prepared by Sanborn. He pointed out that the Cutter-Sanborn three-figure tables were made independently of the two-figure table and could not be used in combination with them, because different numbers would fall to almost every name. Cutter also emphasized the fact that his new table would be handier to use, and would be sold at a lesser price; and for those libraries who already had the two-figure table he would give them a special price if they purchased his new three-figure table![7]

Cutter wrote a small booklet of explanation to accompany his new three-figure table and in it he deliberately ignored mentioning the Cutter-Sanborn table published some six years earlier. In a note he stated:

```
Two sets of tables have been issued:  the first with only 2

figures after the initial; the second with 3 figures.  These

can be used successively in the same class, because the two

figures of the first are the same as the first two figures of

the 3-figure table.⁸
```

Library Bureau had included both the Cutter-Sanborn table and Cutter's two-figure table in the same advertisement until Cutter published his own three-figure table.[9] But, after Cutter's three-figure table was published in 1901, the Library Bureau advertisements no longer included the Cutter-Sanborn table. However, it was mentioned in the description of the new three-figure table. The only explanation is that Cutter felt his was much better and that libraries should use his table and not the one prepared by Sanborn. One advertisement about the three-figure table stated that "these tables are simply an enlargement of the Cutter 2-figure table, and can not

6. *Public libraries* 5 (June 1900): 243.
7. *Library journal* 27 (January 1902): 47; *Public libraries* 7 (February 1902): 57.
8. Cutter, *Explanation of the alphabetic-order marks*, p.3.
9. *Public libraries* 4 (May 1899): 242.

only be employed to better advantage than the Cutter-Sanborn tables, where the 2-figure tables have been used, but they can be worked for both two or three figures equally well."[10]

From 1895 to 1901 the only three-figure table available was that of Sanborn and it was being widely used before Cutter finally came out with his expansion of the original two-figure table. Cutter tried to have his new table replace that of Sanborn, but without any effect. Melvil Dewey used Cutter's two-figure table for author numbers in the examples given in his *Library school rules* until Cutter published Sanborn's expansion. In his *Simplified library school rules* he used the Sanborn expansion. About the Cutter tables Dewey wrote the following:

> The best and most widely used translation system for names
>
> is that devised by Mr. C. A. Cutter. . . .
>
> The first edition of the tables carried the subdivisions
>
> to two figures; in the second edition entitled Alfabetic-order
>
> tables altered and fitted with three figures by Kate E. Sanborn,
>
> the numbers are carried to three figures. The later edition has
>
> been used in the following rules.[11]

As stated earlier, the last quarter of the nineteenth century witnessed the field of librarianship developing and expanding at a great pace: the American Library Association was founded; the first issue of *Library journal* was published; the first library school was started; libraries began to classify their collections and look for ways to improve the organization of library materials; and many new libraries came into being. The American public began to have an interest in the establishment of libraries and more libraries meant more librarians; more librarians meant more persons interested in the profession and its development. One reason for the great surge in the number of libraries in this country was the philanthropy of Andrew Carnegie, who gave "more than $40,000,000 . . . for the erection of 1679 public library buildings in 1412 communities of the United States."[12] These gifts began in 1886 and lasted until 1919.[13] These libraries needed tools such as classification schemes and author tables. During this period there were only two published clas-

10. *Public libraries* 7 (November 1902): 448.

11. Melvil Dewey, *Simplified library school rules* (Boston: Library Bureau, 1898), p. 54. Also _____, "Simplified library school rules," *Library notes* 4 (October 1898): 293.

12. George S. Bobinski, *Carnegie libraries : their history and impact on American public library development* (Chicago: American Library Association, 1969), p. 20.

13. Ibid., p. 13.

sification schemes that were readily available and widely known: Dewey's *Decimal classification* and Cutter's *Expansive classification*. Regardless which one a library might choose, a Cutter table would be needed to sub-arrange the materials by author. In previous years many libraries had found the Cutter two-figure table inadequate. Therefore after the publication of the Cutter-Sanborn table, many librarians purchased it and began to use it in their libraries. By the time Cutter published his three-figure table in 1901 many libraries were already using the Cutter-Sanborn table, including the Library of Congress. The establishment of so many new libraries with the need for library tools made the Cutter-Sanborn table a basic library tool, whose popularity has not diminished in the twentieth century.

At the turn of the century the Library of Congress was developing its own classification scheme and it used as a guide Cutter's *Expansive classification*. The first class to be developed by the Library of Congress was Class Z, Bibliography and Library Science. The Cutter-Sanborn table was used to form the subdivisions of certain classification numbers by "topics." In the "Prefatory note" dated January 1, 1902 of this early edition of the Z schedule it was stated that:

> The order of the main groups, the arrangement under Library
> Science, and many other details not easily specified are, in
> part, from an advance outline (1898) of Cutter's Expansive
> classification. The numbers used for "topics" are from the
> Cutter-Sanborn table.[14]

The following examples of these "topics" from the Z schedule show that the Library of Congress adopted Sanborn's idea of using just one letter followed by digits and not Cutter's method of using two or three letters for names beginning with vowels and the letter S.

7164.C47	Charities
7164.C6	Civil service
7164.C7	Colonies
7164.I7	Insurance
7164.P94	Prices

14. Library of Congress, *Class Z : bibliography and library science* (Washington: Government Printing Office, 1902), p. 3.

```
7164.S66    Social questions

7164.S67    Socialism

7164.T23    Taxation

7164.T87    Trusts

7164.U56    Unemployed
```

After Cutter published his new three-figure table, the Library of Congress did not discontinue the use of the Cutter-Sanborn table, but did adopt and adapt Cutter's three-figure table for fiction. However, the Cutter-Sanborn table remained the guide for all other classes. In her book, *Author notation in the Library of Congress*, published in 1917, Anna Cantrell Laws wrote:

> In the alphabetical arrangement of the Library of Congress
>
> the Cutter three-figure table is used as a basis in assigning
>
> numbers for books in Fiction; the Cutter-Sanborn three-figure
>
> table for all other classes. Neither is strictly adhered to,
>
> and there are numerous exceptions.[15]

The Library of Congress classification is a very close classification and if numbers from either the Cutter-Sanborn table or the Cutter three-figure table were used many call numbers would be unnecessarily long. Therefore the Library of Congress developed its own author number table to be used with its classification schedules. This table follows Cutter's principle of using the initial letter followed by a decimal number representing the remaining letters of the name or term being cuttered. Only the necessary number of digits is used depending on the quantity of materials classified under any particular classification number. Cutter numbers consisting of the initial letter and just one digit are not uncommon. On the other hand, under some classification numbers four or five digits may be required. Thus it is the quantity of materials with the same classification number that dictates the number of digits used with the initial letter. The Library of Congress author number table is very simple and the latest version is given below as it appeared in the Library of Congress *Cataloging service bulletin*.[16]

15. Anna Cantrell Laws, *Author notation in the Library of Congress* (Washington: Government Printing Office, 1917), pp. 5–6.
16. *Cataloging service bulletin* 3 (Winter 1979): 19–20.

BOOK NUMBERS

Library of Congress call numbers consist, in general, of two principal elements: class number and book number, to which are added, as required, symbols designating a particular work.

Library of Congress book numbers are composed of the initial letter of the main entry heading, followed by Arabic numerals representing the succeeding letters on the following basis:

1) After inital vowels

for the second letter:	b	d	l,m	n	p	r	s,t	u-y
use number:	2	3	4	5	6	7	8	9

2) After the initial letter S

for the second letter:	a	ch	e	h,i	m-p	t	u
use number:	2	3	4	5	6	7-8	9

3) After the initial letters Qu

for the third letter:	a	e	i	o	r	y
use number:	3	4	5	6	7	9

for names beginning Qa-Qt

use: 2-29

4) After other initial consonants

for the second letter:	a	e	i	o	r	u	y
use number:	3	4	5	6	7	8	9

5) When an additional number is preferred

for the third letter:	a-d	e-h	i-l	m	n-q	r-t	u-w	x-z
use number:	2*	3	4	5	6	7	8	9

(* optional for third letter a or b)

Letters not included in these tables are assigned the next higher or lower number as required by previous assignments in the particular class.

The arrangements in the following examples illustrate some possible applications of these tables:

1) Names beginning with vowels

Abernathy	.A2	Ames	.A45	Astor	.A84
Adams	.A3	Appleby	.A6	Atwater	.A87

| Aldrich | .A4 | Archer | .A7 | Austin | .A9 |

2) Names beginning with the letter S

Saint	.S2	Simmons	.S5	Steel	.S7
Schaefer	.S3	Smith	.S6	Storch	.S75
Seaton	.S4	Southerland	.S64	Sturges	.S8
Shank	.S45	Springer	.S66	Sullivan	.S9

3) Names beginning with the letters Qu

Qadriri	.Q2	Queist	.Q5	Qureshi	.Q7
Quabbe	.Q3	Quick	.Q6	Quynn	.Q9
Queener	.Q4				

4) Names beginning with other consonants

Carter	.C3(7)	Cinelli	.C5(6)	Cullen	.C8(4)
Cecil	.C4(2)	Corbett	.C6(7)	Cyprus	.C9(6)
Childs	.C45	Croft	.C7(6)		

( ) = if using two numbers

5) When there are no existing conflicting entries in the shelflist,
    the use of a third letter book number may be preferred:

Cabot	.C3	Callahan	.C34	Carter	.C37
Cadmus	.C32	Campbell	.C35	Cavelli	.C38
Caffrey	.C33	Cannon	.C36	Cazalas	.C39

The numbers are decimals, thus allowing for infinite
interpolation of the decimal principle.

Since the tables provide only a general framework for the assignment
of numbers, the symbol for a particular name or work is constant only
within a single class. Each entry must be added to the existing entries
in the shelflist in such a way as to preserve alphabetic order in
accordance with Library of Congress filing rules.

During the first half of the twentieth century there were three manuals of
cataloging and classification which were the most widely read and the most
influential in the United States.[17] Their authors are Theresa Hitchler, Margaret Mann, and Susan Grey Akers.

The first edition of Hitchler's book was published in 1905. In it she recommended only the Cutter-Sanborn table. Hitchler stated very simply and directly: "For book numbers use the Cutter-Sanborn Author tables. . . ."[18] In

17. Donald J. Lehnus, *Milestones in cataloging : famous catalogers and their writings, 1835–1969* (Littleton, Colorado: Libraries Unlimited, 1974), pp. 72–73.

18. Theresa Hitchler, *Cataloging for small libraries*, Library tract, no. 7 (Boston: ALA Publishing Board, 1905), p. 32.

the 1909 edition, and in the second and third editions of 1915 and 1926, she continued to recommend only the Cutter-Sanborn table.[19]

Margaret Mann published the first edition of her cataloging and classification manual in 1928. She made the following comment about author number tables:

> The Cutter 2-figure alphabetic order table is suitable for
>
> libraries of less than 5,000 volumes but should not be purchased
>
> for libraries larger than this. If, however, the 2-figure table
>
> has been used and the library wants to extend it, a Cutter 3-figure
>
> is available which is an enlargement of the 2-figure. The table
>
> usually recommended today is the Cutter-Sanborn 3-figure alphabetic
>
> table, which is an independent scheme, not an enlargement of the
>
> Cutter 2-figure table.[20]

In the 1930 edition and the second edition of 1943 Mann repeated the same idea that the author table "usually recommended" is the Cutter-Sanborn table.[21]

Susan Grey Akers is the only one of these three authors who used Cutter's three-figure table as an example of an author table. In the first edition, which was published in 1927, Akers wrote: "This [book] number is a combination of letters and figures taken from an author table, e.g., Cutter's *Three-figure alphabetic order table*."[22] In all later editions Akers changed this example to the Cutter-Sanborn table and never again mentioned Cutter's three-figure table.[23]

19. Theresa Hitchler, *Cataloging for small libraries*, Library handbook, no. 2 (Chicago: ALA Publishing Board, 1909), p. 32.

————, *Cataloging for small libraries*; Rev. ed. (Chicago: ALA, 1915), p. 271.

————, *Cataloging for small libraries*, 3d enl. ed. (New York: Stechert, 1926), p. 271.

20. Margaret Mann, *The classification and cataloging of books* (Chicago: American Library Association, 1928), p. 115.

21. Margaret Mann, *Introduction to cataloging and the classification of books* (Chicago: American Library Association, 1930), pp. 118–19

————, *Introduction to cataloging and the classification of books*, 2d ed. (Chicago: American Library Association, 1943), p. 89.

22. Susan Grey Akers, *Simple library cataloging* (Chicago: American Library Association, 1927), p. 11.

23. Susan Grey Akers, *Simple library cataloging*, 2d ed. rewritten (Chicago: American Library Association, 1933), p. 16.

————, *Simple library cataloging*, 3d ed. rewritten (Chicago: American Library Association, 1944), p. 15.

————, *Simple library cataloging*, 4th ed. (Chicago: American Library Association, 1954), pp. 20, 23.

There must be a reason why such prominent and widely read authors of cataloging and classification manuals would recommend the Cutter-Sanborn table instead of Cutter's three-figure table. Did Kate Sanborn produce a work so superior to Cutter's that his fell to disuse? A comparison should be made of the three different tables to try to find the reason for the continued popular use of the Cutter-Sanborn table and desuetude of Cutter's three-figure table.

Cutter's two-figure table proved to be inadequate for many libraries even in the nineteenth century so it is not surprising that it is hardly used in the twentieth century.

There is no doubt that the basic reason for the popularity of Sanborn's table is due to the fact that librarians have preferred her idea of using only the initial letter of the name with digits. Cutter believed that the author numbers formed from names beginning with a vowel or the letter S should use two or three letters and not just the initial. Cutter's two-figure table contained the following instructions printed in the margin between the letters I and O.

```
Use one letter for words beginning with consonants (except S),

two for words beginning with vowels or with S, three for words

beginning with Sc.  Ii, Iw, Ix, Iy, Oo, Uo, Uq, Uu, Ss, and

Sx can generally be used without figures.²⁴
```

These same instructions were also printed between the letters I and O in the three-figure table of 1901.²⁵

Sanborn consistently used one letter followed by digits. She used two digits for the letters E, I, O, U, J, K, Y, and Z; one digit for the letters Q and X; for all other letters she provided three digits. Cutter's three-figure table did not hold to any consistency at all. He assigned from one to three digits for all letters of the alphabet except A, E, Q, S, X, Y, and Z, which had one to two digits; the letters I, O, and U were assigned only one digit. For some reason Cutter included the letter X twice in his table, each time with a different set of numbers.

Examples from the two tables will point out basic differences between them.

Cutter's Three-figure table		Sanborn's Three-figure table	
L	1	La	111
La	11	Lab	112
Lab	111	Labar	113

24. Charles Ammi Cutter, *Alfabetic-order table* ([Boston: Library Bureau, 1888]), p. [3].
25. Charles Ammi Cutter, *Three-figure alfabetic-order table* ([Boston: Library Bureau, 1901]), p. [22].

Labau	112		Labat	114
Labi	113		Labbe	115
Labori	114		Labe	116
Labro	115		Labeo	117
Ly	98		Ly	981
Lyau	981		Lycu	982
Lyck	982		Lyd	983
Lyd	983		Lye	984
Lyden	984		Lyl	985
Lydi	985		Lym	986
Lye	986		Lyn	987

Both Cutter and Sanborn realized that many librarians preferred the use of just one letter with digits rather than the two or three letters that Cutter insisted upon in both his two-figure and three-figure tables. In the 1899 edition of the booklet that accompanied the Cutter-Sanborn table, Cutter wrote:

> For names beginning with A, E, I, O, U, and S, I prefer to use the first two letters of the author's name instead of the initial, and for names beginning with Sc three letters.
>
> In my original tables this was provided for, but only one figure was used, the second letter taking the place of a figure. For large classes a second figure is needed, and I am preparing such a table for use at the Forbes Library. Some persons, however, object to the use of two letters. For such Miss Sanborn has prepared a table of the vowels and S with three figures. In the old table, Abbot is AB2, Edwards, ED9, Ives, IV3, Olney OL6, Upton, UP1, Semmes, SE5, Scammon, SCA5, Schopenhauer, SCH6.
>
> In this way fewer marks are used for the same amount of distinction.[26]

26. Charles Ammi Cutter, *Explanation of the Cutter-Sanborn author-marks (three-figure tables)*, 3d ed. (Northampton, Mass.: Herald Office, 1899), p. 4.

The next edition of the same booklet that accompanied the Cutter-Sanborn table was published in 1904, one year after Cutter's death. Sanborn revised the booklet and eliminated the paragraph given above and at the very end of the booklet she added the following comment:

> Libraries which have already used the original two-figure
> table, and wish to expand in certain classes, should use the
> three-figure Cutter table which was made for that purpose. The
> Cutter-Sanborn table was compiled for those who desire a three-
> figure table which carries the same principle into the vowels
> and S; namely, the use of the initial letter of the author's
> name with three figures, instead of the first two letters of
> the name with two figures, which is a feature of the other
> Cutter tables.[27]

Bertha Rickenbrode Barden (1883–   ), author of the popular manual entitled, *Book numbers: a manual for students with a basic code of rules*, also realized that the use of just the initial letter followed by digits made the Cutter-Sanborn table superior to those of Cutter. In her manual she wrote:[28]

> The Cutter-Sanborn table is more satisfactory because of its
> uniform plan. A comparison with the Cutter table illustrates
> this:

Name	Cutter number	Cutter-Sanborn number
Scott, W.	Sco86	S431
Shaw, W.	Sh28	S537
Thayer, S.	T338	T373
Upton	Up8	U71

Besides the preference by librarians for Sanborn's style of author numbers in which only the initial letter was used in conjunction with digits for all letters of the alphabet, there must be other reasons why the Cutter three-

27. Charles Ammi Cutter, *Explanation of the Cutter-Sanborn author-marks (three-figure tables)*, 4th ed., revised by Kate Emery Jones (Boston: Library Bureau, 1904), p. 8.

28. Bertha R. Barden, *Book numbers : a manual for students with a basic code of rules* (Chicago: American Library Association, 1937), pp. 7–8.

figure table has never been as popular as Sanborn's. The following details about the three Cutter tables will attempt to prove why the Cutter-Sanborn table is more widely used than either of Cutter's tables.

The optimal quantity of numbers for an author table may be difficult to ascertain; libraries vary in size and some will need more extensive tables than others. Cutter's two-figure table has less than 3,000 numbers and it was proven inadequate for many libraries even before the end of the nineteenth century. Sanborn's table contains slightly more than 12,000 numbers and Cutter's three-figure table has more than 20,000. Most libraries today use the Cutter-Sanborn table. According to the number of sales of the three Cutter tables two-thirds of those sold are Cutter-Sanborn tables.[29] This indicates that more libraries use this table than any other one. Libraries using Dewey's *Decimal Classification* have found the Cutter-Sanborn table adequate for their needs. From this it can be assumed that an adequate author table for use with Dewey's *Decimal Classification* should contain approximately 12,000 to 15,000 numbers distributed in the correct proportion for each letter of the alphabet. This correct proportion of numbers for names with the same initial letter is undoubtedly more important than the total amount of numbers in the table. A correct proportion will have a perfect correlation *between* the quantity of numbers assigned to each letter of the alphabet *and* the frequency of names beginning with each letter.

How would one determine the correct proportion of numbers to be assigned to each letter of the alphabet for an author table? What sources would give the best results to determine the most adequate distribution of numbers among the twenty-six letters of the alphabet? Would the results of studies done a century ago still be valid today? What did Kate Sanborn and Charles Cutter use when they made their author tables?

In order to answer these questions and to be able to evaluate and compare the three Cutter tables used today, this author turned to two sources, both considered better than anything available in the nineteenth century. The first is the register of names in the files of the Social Security Administration. A report on the distribution of 239,927,977 surnames in the Social Security number file was compiled in 1974.[30] As far as this author can determine this list of almost 240 million names is the largest group ever analyzed to determine the distribution of surnames according to the initial letter.

How accurate would such a list of personal names be for library purposes when one considers that library author catalogs contain both personal and

29. Richard Ammi Cutter, Personal correspondence to the author, September 8, 1979.

30. Social Security Administration, Office of Program Operations, *Report of distribution of surnames in the Social Security number file, September 1, 1974*, BDP Publication no. 034-75 [7-75] ([Washington: The Administration, 1975?]).

corporate names? To attempt to answer this question this author analyzed the names, both personal and corporate, listed in twenty large metropolitan area telephone directories from all parts of the United States.[31]

Table 1 lists the results of the analyses of the names in the telephone directories and of those in the Social Security number files. The letters are in rank order by frequency as determined by the analysis of the telephone directories. The differences are very minute; in fact the mean of the differences of the twenty-six letters is only 0.26, that is, a mean difference of just one-fourth of 1 percent for each letter. The largest difference for any letter is just 1.143 percent and one letter has the small difference of 0.007 percent. It must be remembered that telephone directories contain both personal and corporate names whereas the Social Security files contain only personal names. This would account for the differences in the percentage of names beginning with several of the letters, for example, the letter U has a higher percentage in the telephone directories because of the numerous entries under "United States"; library catalogs also have numerous entries under this heading. Therefore one can assume that the analysis of the telephone directories is slightly more accurate for library purposes.

The "differences" in Tables 1, 2, 3, 4, 6, 7, and 8 are given as absolute values; it is immaterial if the value of each difference is plus or minus.

Even before Cutter was convinced that author numbers should consist of the initial letter followed by digits, there were at least two librarians, Jacob Schwartz and John Edmands, who had attempted to determine the correct distribution of numbers for each letter of the alphabet according to the actual frequency in which names begin with each letter of the alphabet. Schwartz was the first; he distributed the numbers 0 to 999 from A to Z, assigning each letter a certain amount of numbers. Schwartz made two completely different author tables, the first of which was to be used with his "Combined" classification and was described in *Library journal* in 1878.[32] The second one was devised to accompany his "Mnemonic system of classification," of which a preliminary outline appeared in *Library journal* the following year.[33] In 1882 a later version of his "Mnemonic" system was presented in more detail along

31. The telephone directories analyzed were from Atlanta; Baltimore; Chicago; Cincinnati; Denver; Detroit; District of Columbia; Houston; Kansas City; Los Angeles; Manhattan (New York City); Maryland suburban (Washington metropolitan area); Minneapolis; New Orleans; Northern Virginia (Washington metropolitan area); Orange County, California; Philadelphia; Phoenix; Richmond, Virginia; and Westchester and Putnam Counties, New York.

32. Jacob Schwartz, "A 'combined' system for arranging and numbering," *Library journal* 3 (March 1878): 7–8.

33. Jacob Schwartz, "A mnemonic system of classification," *Library journal* 4 (January 1879): [4]–7.

TABLE 1.   Comparison between the Distribution of Names in the Social
Security Files and the Telephone Directories

	Distribution of personal and corporate names from telephone directories	Distribution of personal names from the Social Security Administration records	
	Percent	Percent	Difference
S	10.10	10.088	0.012
M	9.05	9.424	0.374
B	8.65	9.233	0.583
C	7.60	7.336	0.264
H	6.55	7.344	0.794
W	5.80	6.149	0.349
G	5.25	5.175	0.075
R	5.00	5.398	0.398
P	4.80	4.906	0.106
D	4.65	4.823	0.173
L	4.50	4.676	0.176
A	4.30	3.157	1.143
F	3.75	3.590	0.160
K	3.70	3.814	0.114
T	3.50	3.478	0.022
J	2.75	2.927	0.177
N	2.15	1.783	0.367
E	2.10	1.908	0.192
O	1.42	1.452	0.032
V	1.34	1.394	0.054
U	0.90	0.239	0.661
I	0.78	0.402	0.378
Z	0.56	0.548	0.012
Y	0.54	0.566	0.026
Q	0.25	0.186	0.064
X	0.01	0.003	0.007
	100.00	100.00 [sic]	6.713

with the complete author table that was to be used in conjunction with this "Mnemonic" classification.[34]

The author table that he devised for his "Combined" classification was purely an author table, and it not only arranged the books alphabetically, but also divided each letter combination into four groups according to the size of the book, that is, duodecimos, octavos, quartos, and folios. Thus each letter combination had four numbers assigned to it. When Schwartz presented his "Combined system for arranging and numbering" he did not go into detail about the method used for determining the distribution of the numbers among the twenty-six letters, but he did explain how he determined the distribution of numbers to divide each group by size. He said that it was "based on careful calculations made from the statistics of various libraries."[35] He may also have used library statistics for the distribution of numbers for each letter when he assigned the numbers 0 to 999 among the letters of the alphabet. (See Tables 3, 7, 8, and 9.)

Schwartz's second author table created for his "Mnemonic" classification was quite different from the first one.[36] This table had a dual purpose; it was an author table and also served to further subdivide each basic classification number. The distribution of letters was not the same as that used in the first author table. (See Tables 2, 7, 8, and 9.) This new table did not provide for subdividing the books by size as did the first one. For the distribution of the numbers among the letters he used various reference works and catalogs. Schwartz also let it be known that other classificationists had adopted his original plan. About author numbers in general and his own author tables Schwartz wrote the following:

> Having a system of alphabetically arranged classes from A.0 to Z.9, the problem is to unite with them a series of numbers sufficiently large to provide for the probable acquisitions in each class. I have selected 999 as the lowest admissible number. The usual method of numbering the separate works in each class, in the "Movable" system, is to take them in the order of their acquisition and call the first No. 1, the second No. 2, and so on. This is essentially arbitrary, as there is no reason whatever, aside from the mere accident of purchase, why a book should

34. Jacob Schwartz, "A new classification and notation," *Library journal* 7 (July-August 1882): 148–66. The "Alphabetical table of author numbers" is on pages 163–64.
35. Schwartz, "A 'combined' system for arranging and numbering," p. 7.
36. Ibid., pp. 6–10. Also Schwartz, "A new classification and notation," pp. 163–64.

have one number rather than another. As the subject treated
determines the place of each book in a scheme of classification,
it would be more logical and consistent to have the <u>number</u>
conditioned by something in the book itself. It was this consideration which led me, in 1871, to devise my system of alphabetical notation, which forms one of the essential and peculiar
features of my original plan, and which has been adopted with
more or less variation in most of the schemes devised since that
time. . . .

    If we take a number of alphabetically arranged works, such
as Directories, Cyclopedias, and Catalogues, and average the
space occupied by the several letters, we shall find that we
can make nine nearly equal divisions with the following letters:
No. 1 beginning with A, 2 with B, 3 with D, 4 with G, 5 with I,
6 with M, 7 with O, 8 with S, and 9 with T. This scheme of
division is easily remembered, as the vowels A, E, I, O, and U,
have the <u>odd</u> numbers 1, 3, 5, 7, and 9. It not only forms the
basis of the several numbering tables, but has been applied in
numbering the classes. It will, therefore, serve as a <u>mnemonic</u>
<u>key</u> to the whole system, and will enable one to not only give the
class number of every important subject, but to make a pretty
shrewd guess as to the author number.[37]

    Table 2 is a comparison of the two distributions done by Schwartz for his
"Combined" and "Mnemonic" classifications with telephone directory
distributions.[38] The letters are in rank order by distribution in the telephone
directories. The table includes the percentage for each letter in Schwartz's

37. Schwartz, "A new classification and notation," pp. 149–50.
38. The data for the distribution of numbers among the twenty-six letters in Schwartz's first
author table are taken from Edmands's article, "Proportion of initial letters in author
catalogs," *Library journal* 4 (February 1879): 56.

TABLE 2. Comparison of the Distribution of Names in the Two Author
Tables of Schwartz with That of the Telephone Directories

Letters in rank order	Percent	Schwartz (First author table)		Schwartz (Second author table)	
		Percent	Difference	Percent	Difference
S	10.10	10.00	0.10	11.00	0.90
M	9.05	10.00	0.95	9.00	0.05
B	8.65	10.00	1.35	10.00	1.35
C	7.60	8.00	0.40	8.00	0.40
H	6.55	8.00	1.45	6.00	0.55
W	5.80	7.00	1.20	4.70	1.10
G	5.25	4.00	1.25	5.00	0.25
R	5.00	4.00	1.00	4.00	1.00
P	4.80	4.00	0.80	5.70	0.90
D	4.65	4.00	0.65	4.00	0.65
L	4.50	4.00	0.50	6.00	1.50
A	4.30	4.00	0.30	4.00	0.30
F	3.75	4.00	0.25	5.30	1.55
K	3.70	4.00	0.30	2.00	1.70
T	3.50	4.00	0.50	4.00	0.50
J	2.75	2.00	0.75	2.00	0.75
N	2.15	2.00	0.15	2.30	0.15
E	2.10	2.00	0.10	2.00	0.10
O	1.42	1.00	0.42	1.00	0.42
V	1.34	1.00	0.34	1.00	0.34
U	0.90	1.00	0.10	1.00	0.10
I	0.78	1.00	0.22	1.00	0.22
Z	0.56	0.40	0.16	0.30	0.26
Y	0.54	0.40	0.14	0.40	0.14
Q	0.25	0.20	0.05	0.30	0.05
X	0.01	0.00	0.01	0.00	0.01
	100.00	100.00	13.44	100.00	15.24

analyses and the difference in percentage when compared to the names in the telephone directories.

John Edmands used two sources to try to determine the frequency of names beginning with each letter. His first source was Phillips's *Dictionary of biographical reference*.[39] This biographical dictionary contains more than 100,000 names, is international in scope, and covers all periods. Edmands counted the number of names under each letter of the alphabet and made a distribution table for each letter.[40]

Edmands's other source was arrived at by averaging the number of authors' names beginning with the same letter which were found in five library author catalogs. (See Tables 3, 7, 8, and 9.) He calculated the percentage of names for each letter of the alphabet and determined the proportion of numbers needed for each letter.[41]

Another librarian who also used Phillips's *Dictionary of biographical reference* for the same purpose was Ernest Cushing Richardson (1860–1939) of the Princeton College Library. Richardson explained that when a library wants author numbers consisting of only digits and not letters or mixed characters the librarian should "take Phillips' 'Dictionary of Biographical Reference'; divide into something less than 9000 parts by marking off every twelve names. Then put on the consecutive number, and the table is ready made. . . . This makes about as close an approximation as can be to a general list to fit all cases. For special classes it is recommended that special tables be made by taking the longest available list of authors in that class and mathematically adapting."[42]

Table 3 compares the two analyses of Edmands with the distribution of names in the telephone directories. His first analysis is five library author catalogs, and the second is Phillips's *Dictionary of biographical reference*. Letters are in rank order by their frequency in the telephone directories. The table gives the percentage for each letter in Edmands's analysis and the difference in percentage when compared to the names in the telephone directories.

A. P. Massey, librarian of the Case Library in Cleveland, also tried to determine the correct distribution of numbers for each letter of the alphabet. (See Tables 4, 7, 8, and 9.) He only gave his source of data as "biographical

39. Lawrence Barnett Phillips, *The dictionary of biographical reference : containing one hundred thousand names, together with a classed index of the biographical literature of Europe and America* (London: Sampson Low, Son & Marston, 1871).

40. John Edmands, "Proportion of initial letters in author catalogs," *Library journal* 4 (February 1879): 56.

41. Ibid.

42. Ernest Cushing Richardson, "An expansive author-table," *Library journal* 18 (June 1893): 187.

TABLE 3.   Comparison of the Distribution of Names in the Two Studies of Edmands and the Telephone Directories

Letters in rank order	Percent	Edmands (Five catalogs)		Edmands (Phillips' Dictionary)	
		Percent	Difference	Percent	Difference
S	10.10	10.20	0.10	7.50	2.60
M	9.05	9.00	0.05	7.50	1.55
B	8.65	9.40	0.75	12.80	4.15
C	7.60	8.10	0.50	9.50	1.90
H	6.55	6.30	0.25	4.80	1.75
W	5.80	4.70	1.10	3.60	2.20
G	5.25	5.00	0.25	5.70	0.45
R	5.00	4.50	0.50	4.60	0.40
P	4.80	7.00	2.20	5.50	0.70
D	4.65	4.40	0.25	5.00	0.35
L	4.50	5.20	0.70	5.60	1.10
A	4.30	4.40	0.10	7.90	3.60
F	3.75	3.50	0.25	3.80	0.05
K	3.70	1.60	2.10	1.60	2.10
T	3.50	4.10	0.60	2.80	0.70
J	2.75	2.00	0.75	1.70	1.05
N	2.15	2.30	0.15	1.90	0.25
E	2.10	2.50	0.40	2.30	0.20
O	1.42	1.50	0.08	1.60	0.18
V	1.34	1.50	0.16	2.10	0.76
U	0.90	0.90	0.00	0.30	0.60
I	0.78	0.90	0.12	0.60	0.18
Z	0.56	0.30	0.26	0.80	0.24
Y	0.54	0.30	0.24	0.20	0.34
Q	0.25	0.30	0.05	0.25	0.00
X	0.01	0.10	0.09	0.05	0.04
	100.00	100.00	12.00	100.00	27.44

dictionaries." He distributed the numbers 1 through 934 from A to Z and published his results in 1881 with an explanation of how his system of numbers could be used to subarrange books by his "author numbers."[43]

Table 4 compares the distribution of names by Massey based on his study of biographical dictionaries with the telephone directories. Letters are in rank order by frequency as determined by the analysis of the telephone directories. The table gives the percentage for each letter in Massey's analysis and the difference in percentage when compared to the names in the telephone directories.

At this point it should be stressed that a basic difference between Cutter's book numbers and those of Schwartz, Edmands, and Massey is that Cutter's numbers are decimals while the book numbering plans of the other three use integers. Another basic difference is that both Cutter and Sanborn approached the entire distribution problem quite differently than Schwartz, Edmands, and Massey had done. The latter three compiled their tables with a predetermined quantity of digits to be distributed among the twenty-six letters. Cutter and Sanborn apparently predesigned the letter combinations and then assigned the necessary quantity of numbers to these letter combinations.

No one knows what Sanborn used to determine her letter combinations and the quantity of combinations that would be needed for each of the twenty-six letters. Her distribution differs quite radically from that of Cutter's two-figure table (see Table 5). No written records exist to indicate what she used to determine the letter combinations and the distribution of numbers for her table.

Cutter, also, left no record of how he determined the letter combinations necessary for each letter and how many numbers would be needed for each. He seems not to have been very concerned with the quantity of numbers required for each letter of the alphabet according to the frequency of names beginning with each letter. None of his writings indicates that he had any interest in this aspect of the problem. Cutter consulted the catalogs of the Bodleian Library, the Boston Public Library, and the Boston Athenaeum to attempt to determine the possible letter combinations that should be included in an author table. He seems to have been far more concerned with all possible letter combinations than with the correct proportion of numbers for each letter. Another concern of Cutter was the fact that many authors often have the same last name, or names that are so close that an author table would designate the same number for two or more authors. Cutter voiced these concerns at the library symposium on book numbers in 1879 when he stated:

43. A. P. Massey, "Classification of fiction," *Library journal* 6 (January 1881): 7–9.

TABLE 4.   Comparison of the Distribution of Names as Determined by
Massey with That of the Analysis of the Telephone Directories

Letters in rank order	Percent	Massey	
		Percent	Difference
S	10.10	10.06	0.04
M	9.05	8.89	0.16
B	8.65	8.57	0.08
C	7.60	8.57	0.97
H	6.55	8.57	2.02
W	5.80	6.00	0.20
G	5.25	4.28	0.97
R	5.00	4.71	0.29
P	4.80	6.42	1.62
D	4.65	4.39	0.26
L	4.50	5.57	1.07
A	4.30	4.60	0.30
F	3.75	3.10	0.65
K	3.70	1.92	1.78
T	3.50	4.18	0.68
J	2.75	2.14	0.61
N	2.15	1.92	0.23
E	2.10	1.93	0.17
O	1.42	1.82	0.40
V	1.34	0.96	0.38
U	0.90	0.21	0.69
I	0.78	0.54	0.24
Z	0.56	0.11	0.45
Y	0.54	0.32	0.22
Q	0.25	0.11	0.14
X	0.01	0.11	0.10
	100.00	100.00	14.72

The advantage in point of capacity of the letters over figures

for the author notation may be easily overestimated by those who

do not remember that altho all combinations of figures are possible,

many combinations of letters are not. Any letter can begin a

name, it is true, but not every letter can go on with it. So

that, tho the base of the alfabetical notation is 26, the second

story is much smaller. Thus B is followed only by a, e, h, i, j,

l, o, r, u, y. The second letter, if a vowel, may be followed by

any of the 26 letters (tho certain combinations are rare); but

Bl and Br are followed only by the 6 vowels. Many other letters

are limited in the same way....[44]

Table 5 lists in alphabetical order the numbers and percentages given each letter of the alphabet by Cutter and Sanborn in their tables. The data concerning Cutter's two-figure table are all taken from the 1888 revised edition. This edition was chosen for the statistical comparisons because it was the third and final revision of the two-figure table and the one used for the longest period of time. The 1880 edition is not available and it was only a preliminary version; the 1886 edition was only in print for about two or three years.

Table 6 gives the percentages of the numbers assigned to each letter of the alphabet by Cutter and Sanborn in the rank order of the letters as determined by the analysis of the telephone directories. Also given are the differences for each letter when the percentages between each table and the telephone directories are compared.

Table 7 tabulates in rank order the mean of the differences for each analysis done by the Social Security Administration, Edmands, Schwartz, Massey, and the three Cutter tables when each is compared to the names in the telephone directories. Table 8 gives the range of differences including the largest and smallest variations between the letters in each of the nine distributions in Tables 1, 2, 3, 4, and 6 when compared to the distribution of names in the telephone directories.

The data presented in Tables 1, 7, and 8 clearly point out the similarity between the distribution of names in the Social Security files and the tele-

---

44. Charles Ammi Cutter, "Plans for numbering, with especial reference to fiction : a library symposium," *Library journal* 4 (February 1879): 44–45.

TABLE 5. Quantities and Percentages of the Numbers Assigned to Each Letter of the Alphabet in the Three Cutter Tables

	Cutter-Sanborn		Cutter's 2-figure		Cutter's 3-figure	
	Numbers	Percent	Numbers	Percent	Numbers	Percent
A	729	5.9	234	8.58	2,132	10.2
B	729	5.9	81	2.97	811	3.9
C	729	5.9	81	2.97	811	3.9
D	729	5.9	81	2.97	811	3.9
E	81	0.7	234	8.58	2,132	10.2
F	729	5.9	81	2.97	811	3.9
G	729	5.9	81	2.97	811	3.9
H	729	5.9	81	2.97	811	3.9
I	81	0.7	198	7.26	198	1.0
J	81	0.7	81	2.97	807	3.8
K	81	0.7	81	2.97	802	3.8
L	729	5.9	81	2.97	811	3.9
M	729	5.9	81	2.97	811	3.9
N	729	5.9	81	2.97	811	3.9
O	81	0.7	225	8.25	225	1.1
P	729	5.9	81	2.97	811	3.9
Q	9	0.1	9	0.33	69	0.3
R	729	5.9	81	2.97	811	3.9
S	729	5.9	297	10.90	2,706	13.0
T	729	5.9	81	2.97	811	3.9
U	81	0.7	207	7.59	207	1.0
V	729	5.9	81	2.97	803	3.8
W	729	5.9	81	2.97	811	3.9
X	9	0.1	9	0.33	57	0.3
Y	81	0.7	9	0.33	90	0.4
Z	81	0.7	9	0.33	90	0.4
	12,330	100.0	2,727	100.0	20,861	100.0

TABLE 6. Comparison of the Distribution of Names in the Three Cutter Tables with That of the Telephone Directories

Letters in rank order	Cutter-Sanborn table			Cutter's 3-figure table		Cutter's 2-figure table	
	Percent	Percent	Difference	Percent	Difference	Percent	Difference
S	10.10	5.9	4.20	13.0	2.98	10.90	1.52
M	9.05	5.9	3.15	3.9	8.13	2.97	6.08
B	8.65	5.9	2.75	3.9	4.75	2.97	5.68
C	7.60	5.9	1.70	3.9	8.45	2.97	4.63
H	6.55	5.9	0.65	3.9	2.65	2.97	3.58
W	5.80	5.9	0.10	3.9	4.55	2.97	2.83
G	5.25	5.9	0.65	3.9	1.35	2.97	2.28
R	5.00	5.9	0.90	3.9	1.10	2.97	2.03
P	4.80	5.9	1.10	3.9	0.90	2.97	1.83
D	4.65	5.9	1.25	3.9	0.75	2.97	1.68
L	4.50	5.9	1.40	3.9	0.60	2.97	1.53
A	4.30	5.9	1.60	10.2	5.90	8.58	4.28
F	3.75	5.9	2.15	3.9	0.15	2.97	0.78
K	3.70	0.7	3.00	3.8	0.10	2.97	0.73
T	3.50	5.9	2.40	3.9	0.40	2.97	0.53
J	2.75	0.7	2.05	3.8	1.05	2.97	0.22
N	2.15	5.9	3.75	3.9	1.75	2.97	0.82
E	2.10	0.7	1.40	10.2	8.10	8.58	6.48
O	1.42	0.7	0.72	1.1	0.32	8.25	6.83
V	1.34	0.7	0.64	3.8	2.46	2.97	1.63
U	0.90	0.7	0.20	1.0	0.10	7.59	6.69
I	0.78	0.7	0.08	1.0	0.22	7.26	6.48
Z	0.56	0.7	0.14	0.4	0.16	0.33	0.23
Y	0.54	0.7	0.16	0.4	0.14	0.33	0.21
Q	0.25	0.1	0.15	0.3	0.05	0.33	0.08
X	0.01	0.1	0.09	0.3	0.29	0.33	0.32
	100.00	100.0	36.38	100.00	57.40	100.00	69.98

TABLE 7. Mean of the Differences of the Twenty-Six Letters of Each Distribution When Compared to the Analysis of the Telephone Directories

Source	Mean
1. Social Security files	0.26
2. Edmands (five catalogs)	0.46
3. Schwartz (first author table)	0.52
4. Massey	0.57
5. Schwartz (second author table)	0.59
6. Edmands (Phillips)	1.06
7. Sanborn	1.40
8. Cutter (3-figure table)	2.21
9. Cutter (2-figure table)	2.70

phone directories. *If* an analysis of almost 240 million names will give a correct proportion of all names that begin with each letter of the alphabet, and *if* the results of the analysis of the telephone directories is slightly more accurate for library purposes because it takes into account both personal and corporate names, *then* it can be assumed that the following statements and conclusions are true.

By comparing any list showing the distribution of names beginning with each of the twenty-six letters with the distribution based on the analysis of the telephone directories the degree of accuracy of any such list can be determined.

The analyses by Schwartz and Edmands were done before any Cutter table was ever created, and Cutter and Sanborn knew of the studies and had seen them, but a comparison of the data in Tables 7 and 9 shows that neither Cutter nor Sanborn made a very realistic distribution. It is obvious from this that they did not utilize the information which had already been compiled. Of the three Cutter tables the one by Sanborn has the best distribution of numbers for the letters than either one of Cutter's own tables. Why they did not take advantage of the information so readily available to them remains a mystery.

The data presented in Tables 7 and 8 indicate that the use of library author catalogs, biographical dictionaries, and other such reference works results in a distribution much more in line with reality than anything that may have been used by Cutter or Sanborn. Cutter was so concerned with the possible

TABLE 8. Range of the Differences for Each Distribution When Compared to the Analysis of the Telephone Directories

Source	Range	Largest	Smallest
1. Social Security files	1.36	1.143	0.007
2. Schwartz (first author table)	1.44	1.45	0.01
3. Schwartz (second author table)	1.69	1.70	0.01
4. Massey	1.98	2.02	0.04
5. Edmands (five catalogs)	2.20	2.20	0.00
6. Edmands (Phillips)	3.60	3.60	0.00
7. Sanborn	4.11	4.20	0.09
8. Cutter (2-figure table)	6.75	6.83	0.08
9. Cutter (3-figure table)	8.05	8.10	0.05

letter combinations that he paid little attention (if any at all) to the overall distribution of names beginning with the same letter. Regardless of the fact that Schwartz, Edmands, and Massey had a better idea of how the numbers should be distributed among the twenty-six letters, it must be borne in mind that Cutter and Sanborn are the ones who actually compiled and published author tables which were and still are widely used by libraries. The tables of Schwartz, Edmands, and Massey were never widely used and are now all but forgotten, but yet their distributions of numbers for each letter, which were based on the frequency of names beginning with each letter, were far superior to those of Cutter and Sanborn.

A perusal of the data in Table 6 points out that the Cutter table with the most inferior distribution is Cutter's two-figure table. It has a mean difference of 2.7 for each letter. If one studies this table closely it can be seen that the letters with the largest differences are the five vowels and the letters B, C, and M. Table 9 gives the percentages of numbers that each person had distributed to the five vowels. When Cutter assigned numbers to his predetermined letter combinations for the five vowels it resulted that more than 40 percent of the total quantity of numbers in his two-figure table were assigned to the five vowels. According to the analysis of the telephone directories the vowels should have no more than 9.5 percent of the numbers.

No one can be sure how Cutter arrived at these distributions, but it was either due to the fact that he calculated the possible letter combinations with the vowels which, of course, would be very high; or he may have been basing his distribution on the frequency of the vowels as they are used in the words of a normal English text. It does not seem plausible that Cutter would have

TABLE 9.   Percentages for the Five Vowels in the Ten Distributions

Vowels	Telephone directories	Social Security	Cutter 2-figure	Cutter 3-figure	Sanborn	Schwartz*	Massey	Edmands (5 catalogs)	Edmands (Phillips)
A	4.30	3.157	8.58	10.2	5.9	4.0	4.60	4.4	7.9
E	2.10	1.908	8.58	10.2	0.7	2.0	1.93	2.5	2.3
I	0.78	0.402	7.26	1.0	0.7	1.0	0.54	0.9	0.6
O	1.42	1.452	8.25	1.1	0.7	1.0	1.82	1.5	1.6
U	0.90	0.239	7.59	1.0	0.7	1.0	0.21	0.9	0.3
Totals	9.50	7.158	40.26	23.5	8.7	9.0	9.10	10.2	12.7

*The distributions for the vowels in both author tables devised by Schwartz are identical. This column of figures represents both author tables.

confused the frequency of the letters in a text with the frequency of letters with which personal and corporate names begin, but it is quite coincidental that Cutter assigned 40.26 percent of the numbers to the five vowels, and these same five vowels account for 40 percent of all the letters in a long English text.[45]

It is hard to believe that Cutter did not utilize the studies done previously, and just as incredible is the fact that he never seems to have done any of his own. If he had done any kind of analysis such as Edmands did with the five library author catalogs, Cutter would never have made such a serious error in assigning so many numbers for the vowels.

Cutter did change the percentage of numbers for several of the letters when he made his three-figure table. He raised the percentage of numbers for the letters A and E, and drastically reduced the percentage for the letters I, O, and U. An examination of Table 9 shows that the range of differences between the largest and the smallest is 33.102, but if Cutter's two-figure and three-figure tables are excluded the range drops to 5.542. Everybody made a better distribution of the vowels than did Cutter!

A comparison of the three Cutter tables in Table 5 points out that the Cutter-Sanborn table has only 60 percent of the numbers that Cutter has in his three-figure table, yet Sanborn made a much better distribution of the numbers for her table. This may have contributed greatly to its more wide-spread use than either of Cutter's tables. When Cutter expanded his two-figure table in 1901 he did little more than increase the quantity of numbers eightfold, and to change the percentage of some of the letters. He increased the percentage for all letters except I, O, U, Q, and X. The vowels I, O, and U were greatly decreased and the consonants Q and X were just barely reduced.

The foregoing tables and the information about them definitely prove the superiority of the Cutter-Sanborn table over Cutter's two-figure and three-figure tables. In view of this it is not surprising that the Cutter-Sanborn table is by far the most widely used in libraries which classify with Dewey's *Decimal classification*.

The three Cutter tables always had a very illogical and impractical arrangement. They all began with the consonants and had the vowels and the letter S at the end. Cutter's two-figure table began with the consonants B through W except Q, S, X, Y, and Z. The letters that followed the W were arranged in this order: A, E, I, O, Q, U, X, Y, Z, and S. The three-figure table was similar in arrangement except that the letter X was listed twice; the first position of the X was split, X to Xh preceded Ua; and following Uzy, the remaining combinations Xi to Xyu were listed. The second time that X was

---

45. Frank Higenbottam, *Codes and ciphers* (London: St. Paul's House, 1973), p. 150.

given it was placed between Q and Y, and the numbers assigned to the second X listing were completely different. Cutter never mentioned or explained the two different sets of numbers for the letter X in his booklet that accompanied the three-figure table.[46] The other basic difference is that the letters Q, X, Y, and Z followed the letter S; in the two-figure table they were intercalated in the vowels.

The Cutter-Sanborn table varied just slightly; it also began with the consonants B through W, except S. The letters A, E, I, O, S, and U followed the letter W. The Cutter-Sanborn table is also the only one which was originally published as two separate tables; a table containing the vowels and S was published in 1892, and the other table with the other twenty consonants except S came out three years later in 1895.

Another confusing feature of the three tables was that one column of figures was shared by two columns of letters in almost all cases, and the columns on either side of the numbers represented two different letters. For example:

Bly	661	Coch	Boui	761	Conte	Brist	861	Courl
Bo	662	Cochin	Bouil	762	Conti	Brit	862	Court
Bob	663	Cochr	Boul	763	Conto	Bro	863	Courts
Bod	664	Cock	Boull	764	Contr	Brock	864	Courti
Bock	665	Cockb	Boun	765	Contu	Broe	865	Courtn

Librarians owe much to Esther M. Swift, editor of the H. R. Huntting Company, who greatly improved the arrangement and format of the Cutter tables. In the late 1960s Swift rearranged the Cutter tables giving each column of letters its own column of numbers and arranged the twenty-six letters in a strictly alphabetical order A to Z with no exceptions. Swift acquired the assistance of Paul K. Swanson, who at that time was cataloger at the Forbes Library, Northampton, Massachusetts, and presently is cataloger at the Brockton (Mass.) Public Library. About this task of revising the Cutter tables Swanson says:

As one who suffered through the poor typography, the illogical

arrangement and the many errors of earlier editions I was happy

to lend my support and work with her [Esther M. Swift] in the

project. We devoted a good part of our time to rewriting the

46. Cutter, *Explanation of the alphabetic-order marks.*

instruction booklets. Here my experience in practical cataloging
was useful. When it came to choosing a typeface and the actual
layout of the numbers Esther's past experience and expertise
came to the fore.[47]

The instruction booklet which accompanied the revised tables stated:

This edition of the table has been edited and revised (1969)
for the present owner [Richard Ammi Cutter, 1902- , grandson
of Charles Ammi Cutter] by Paul K. Swanson of the Forbes Library,
Northampton, Massachusetts, and Mrs. Esther M. Swift, Editor of The
H. R. Huntting Company, Inc., distributors of the tables for the
owner. The table appears in a new typeface. Rearrangement into
a single, consecutive alphabet should make the table easier to
use. This edition may be employed in conjunction with earlier
editions, because individual letter and figure combinations have
not been changed, save for the correction of a few typographical
errors.[48]

Catalogers who have used the previous editions of the tables greatly
appreciate the Swanson-Swift revisions of 1969. They are now much easier to
read and their use is greatly facilitated by the new arrangement in a consecutive alphabetical arrangement with just one column of letters for each column of numbers. Unfortunately no one reviewed or wrote an article about
the revisions of these important classification tools. The only item that did
appear was a small notice in *Booklist* in 1970 which reads:

The three Cutter author tables for assigning numbers for arrangement of books are available in a new edition in which each table
is arranged in a single consecutive alphabet. Lightweight but
sturdy covers and a metal spiral binding add to the convenience

47. Paul K. Swanson, Personal correspondence to the author, August 31, 1979.
48. Paul K. Swanson, and Esther M. Swift, *Instruction booklet for Cutter-Sanborn three-figure author table (Swanson-Swift revision, 1969)* (Chicopee, Mass.: H. R. Huntting, 1969), p. [2].

```
of use.  An instruction book accompanies each table.  The three

tables are available only from H. R. Huntting Company, 300 Burnett

Rd., Chicopee, MA 01020.  C. A. Cutter's Two-figure author table

(Swanson-Swift rev., 1969) is $8 net.  C. A. Cutter's Three-figure

author table (Swanson-Swift rev., 1969) is $12 net.  Cutter-

Sanborn Three-figure author table (Swanson-Swift rev., 1969)

is $10 net.⁴⁹
```

The three Cutter tables have always remained available since they were first printed and distributed by Cutter and the Library Bureau of Boston. Library Bureau was the supplier and the distributor of the tables from 1890 to 1946. In 1946 the H. R. Huntting Company of Springfield, Massachusetts, took over the distribution and it remained the distributor until 1979 when Libraries Unlimited of Littleton, Colorado, assumed this responsibility.

Since the publication of Cutter's three-figure table in 1901, very little has been written about book numbers. The most popular and best known publication is that of Bertha Barden which was published by the American Library Association in 1937.[50] This booklet was useful but not completely satisfactory. In the introduction to a pamphlet on book numbers published in Australia in 1977 the authors gave the following as one of their reasons for writing the pamphlet: "There was no totally satisfactory book numbering scheme available. The best known system, developed by Bertha Barden in her *Book numbers* (Chicago, 1937), was outdated, not comprehensive, and not completely logical. So a decision was made to devise a local system, using the Cutter-Sanborn *Three-figure author tables* as a basis."[51]

Author numbers and the various tables devised by librarians interested in classification have had a very fascinating history and it cannot be said that there was any one person who "invented" them, but rather that their evolution and development were due to the roles played by four leading men and a single leading lady, namely, Charles Cutter, Melvil Dewey, John Edmands, Jacob Schwartz, and Kate Sanborn.

In 1881 Melvil Dewey wrote:

```
    Several important schemes are using figures to represent the

    alphabetical order of names.  Great advantages would result if
```

49. *Booklist* 66 (February 15, 1970): 716.
50. Barden, *Book numbers : a manual for students with a basic code of rules.*
51. La Trobe University Library, Technical Services Division, *Book numbers guide*, Library publication, No. 13 (Bundoora, Australia: The Library, 1977), p. iv.

all these schemes could be made uniform, carried to five or more

places, and printed for uniform use. Each library could use one

or more figures, as its wants required. It would save endless

labor and mistakes, and would be a great convenience if there were

such a standard table for translating names into figures. We

suggest a conference of the head translators, Messrs. Massey,

Cutter, Schwartz, etc., at Washington, to settle disputed points

and agree upon a table to be adopted and printed as the standard.[52]

No such meeting ever took place, but the Cutter tables did become the "standard"; they have remained so for the past one hundred years, and they will probably continue to be the standard long into the future.

Summary and Conclusions

During the last quarter of the nineteenth century librarianship had more developments and advanced further than ever before. A major development during this period was classification. There were many debates and much discussion about the classification schemes which were being developed at that time. Dewey was advocating the use of his *Decimal classification*; Cutter was hard at work on his *Expansive classification*; and Schwartz was devising his "Combined" and "Mnemonic" classification schemes. These same men were also interested in the subarrangement of books with the same classification number. Book numbers had an evolution that was coeval with that of the classification schemes, and reached their maturity before the end of the nineteenth century. Schwartz's classification schemes are all but forgotten. Cutter's *Expansive classification* exists today only in those aspects which were adapted into the Library of Congress classification scheme. Dewey's *Decimal classification* has become almost a standard the world over and is still developing and growing stronger. Cutter's author numbers have become the standard for subarranging books with the same classification number in libraries which use the *Decimal classification*. Also, the Library of Congress classification uses Cutter's idea and basic principle of author numbers for subarranging materials.

Two different three-figure tables were developed in a period of less than ten years. Sanborn's expansion of the two-figure table was first published in two separate volumes; the first consisting of just the vowels and the letter S

52. Melvil Dewey, "Note," *Library journal* 6 (January 1881): 9.

came out in 1892, and the second with the consonants except S was printed and distributed in 1895. Cutter's own expansion of the two-figure table first appeared in 1901. Cutter had been so displeased with Sanborn's work that he felt that he had to make another three-figure table based on the numbers in his original table. He attempted to discredit Sanborn's work and to establish his own three-figure table as the standard author number table, but he was unable to do so. The Library of Congress used the Cutter-Sanborn table as the guide in the formation of its author number system and in the method for subarranging topics in its classification scheme.

Sanborn's table was also the one highly recommended by three famous authors of cataloging and classification manuals, Hitchler, Akers, and Mann.

Undoubtedly, the one single factor that has made the Cutter-Sanborn table the preferred one is her idea of the consistent use of just one letter followed by digits. From the very beginning librarians objected to Cutter's preference for two or three letters followed by digits for those names beginning with vowels and the letter S.

Neither Cutter nor Sanborn distributed the numbers among the letters in a very accurate proportion, but Sanborn's distribution is quite superior to that in either of Cutter's two tables. For some unknown reason Cutter and Sanborn did not take advantage of work previously done by other librarians who were interested in author numbers and had made valuable and worthwhile analyses of the distribution of names according to the initial letter.

Regardless of the faults that can be found in the Cutter tables, they are still better than anything else that has been developed thus far and continue to be the standard tools for assigning book numbers.

PART
TWO

Guidelines and Principles
for Assigning Book Numbers

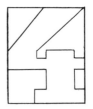

General Principles

The classification number and the book number differ. The classification number is a fixed number because the same number is consistently used for all materials on the same subject. The book number is relative because the number given an author is always in relation to the other book numbers of all the other materials already assigned the same classification number. Thus book numbers for materials written by the same author may vary from one classification number to another. The basic purpose of the book number is to position each new item in its appropriate place in relation to all other materials which have been assigned the same classification number. If there are only a few items with the same classification number the book number can be simple, but if the library has many items classified under one number, then it must be more detailed. The book numbers for large collections classified under the same number or for the works of prolific authors with the same classification number may consist of other letters and numbers representing titles, editors, dates or any other significant factor that is used to make each call number distinctive.

The four basic purposes of book numbers are to:

1. Subarrange the materials with the same classification number in a systematic and logical order.
2. Assign to each item a distinctive group of symbols, that is, a call number, that will distinguish it from all others in the collection.
3. Provide a call number that facilitates finding a particular item among all the others in the collection and returning it to the same relative location.

4. Maintain an accurate record of loaned items, or items that are temporarily away from their normal position, such as books placed in a reserve reading collection or that have been sent to the bindery.

The complexity of book numbers varies from library to library depending on: (1) the type of library (i.e., whether it be a special, public, academic, or school library) and its clientele; and (2) the size and nature of the library's collection. Indubitably, academic and special libraries, or any other maintaining a collection for research and scholarly studies, will need to have more detailed and complex book numbers to differentiate between the various editions and versions of works. School and small public libraries can function very well with much simpler book numbers. In fact, there are many such libraries where works of fiction make up a large proportion of their collections, and usually the fiction collection is arranged alphabetically by author with no call number whatsoever.

Each library has to establish a policy determining how detailed the book numbers need to be. This policy must not be based on the present collection alone, but also on the size that the collection may be in the future. The guidelines outlined in this manual are designed to serve as a basis for constructing book numbers, and they can be adapted easily to the necessities of any type and/or size of library.

All examples of book numbers used in this manual are from the 1969 Swanson-Swift revision of the Cutter-Sanborn three-figure author table.[1] The classification numbers are from the nineteenth edition (1979) of the *Dewey decimal classification*.[2] Even though the guidelines given here may be used with almost any classification scheme, the *Dewey decimal classification* was chosen for the examples because the majority of libraries which assign book numbers from a Cutter table do indeed use this classification scheme. Also, each group of examples in the following chapters is arranged in shelflist order, unless otherwise stated.

In forming book numbers one must remember the basic purpose is to situate each item in its proper relation to all other items already in the collection, as well as to provide for those that may be added to the collection at a later date.

There are three rudiments which must be followed in the formation of book numbers:

1. It is necessary to consult the shelflist before assigning a book number in order to avoid the problem of having different publica-

1. Charles Ammi Cutter, *Cutter-Sanborn three-figure table*, Swanson-Swift revision, 1969 (Chicopee, Mass.: H. R. Huntting Co., 1969) [Distributed by Libraries Unlimited, Inc., Littleton, Colorado].

2. Melvil Dewey, *Dewey decimal classification and relative index*, 19th ed., edited under the direction of Benjamin A. Custer (Albany, N.Y.: Forest Press, 1979).

tions with identical call numbers. Also, by consulting the shelflist it is easier to assign the simplest, but yet the most appropriate book number in relation to all other materials already classified with the same classification number.

2. The length and detail of each book number depends on the number of items with the same classification number. Thus, if there are many items with the same classification number the book number will necessarily have to be longer and more detailed.

3. Book numbers are always considered as decimals. In this way, new numbers can be intercalated indefinitely and an alphabetical order is always maintained.

The most commonly accepted method of arranging materials under the same classification number is alphabetically according to the main entry, albeit a surname, given name, pseudonym, title of a work, uniform title, or corporate name.

Examples:

025.47
C454
	Chan, Lois Mai
	    Library of Congress subject headings :
	    principles and application.

370.193
U58
	U.S. Office of Education.
	    Education for better living : the role of
	    the school in community improvement.

378.7977
U58
	University of Washington.
	    The vision on the knoll, 1861-1961 : the
	    first hundred years of the University of
	    Washington.

499.4 P979	Pukui, Mary Kawena Hawaiian-English dictionary.
614.073 K16	Kansas. Division of Maternal and Child Health. Manual for public health nurses.

615.8424
Q6
	Quimby, Edith H.
	    Radioactive isotopes in medicine and
	    biology.

641.692 G646	Good Housekeeping Institute. Fish and shellfish.
641.692 K21	Kaufman, William Irving The fish and shellfish cookbook.
641.692 S764	The Sportsman's cookbook for the fisherman.

809.3876
L521
	LeGuin, Ursula K.
	    The language of the night : essays
	    on fantasy and science fiction.

813.4
K19
	Kate, Cousin
	    Kenneth and Hugh : or Self-mastery,
	    by Cousin Kate.

823.2
R655
	Robin Hood.
	    Robin Hood's garland : being a complete
	    history of all the notable and merry
	    exploits performed by him and his men
	    on many occasions.

940.5347
B774
	Bourke-White, Margaret
	    Shooting the Russian War, written and
	    photographed by Margaret Bourke-White.

Surnames that begin with the prefixes M', Mc, and Mac (e.g., M'Clintock, McPherson, MacAllister) are treated as though they were written Macclintock, Macpherson, and Macallister. Those that begin with other prefixes or particles such as D', O', El, La, De, and so forth (e.g., O'Neill, El-Wahil, LaFollette, De Valera, D'Annunzio) are treated as though written Oneill, Elwahil, Lafollette, Devalera, and Dannunzio.
Examples:

595.771 L129	La Casse, Walter J. Mosquitoes of Japan.
811.4 D489	De Vere, Mary Ainge Love songs and other poems.
821.4 D196	D'Anvers, Alicia The Oxford-act : a poem.

929.2
M128
	McClure, Mabel Byron
	    The McClures, the Kennedys,
	    the Tennants, the Gays.

972.9105 O36	O'Hagan, Anne Cuba at a glance.

When any name or word falls in between two numbers of the table the first is always used. But it should be remembered that the decisive and determining factor is made by consulting the shelflist to make sure there will be no conflict with any other call number already assigned. Book numbers are always treated as decimals; therefore, there is always room for endless expansion. In order to insert a number between two call numbers already established the digit 5 is added to the first, thus there will remain four unused book numbers on either side of the new number.
Example:

```
540          Sanderson, Emily
S215              Chemistry in action.

540          Sanderson, Mary Ellen
S2155            Introduction to modern chemistry.

540          Sanderson, Robert Thomas
S216             Principles of chemistry.
```

In the above example it can be seen that the first book to be classified was that of Robert Thomas Sanderson because the Cutter-Sanborn table gives 216 as the number for Sanderson; the second book was that of Emily Sanderson and the third one was by Mary Ellen Sanderson. Emily Sanderson's book was acquired after Robert Sanderson's had already been assigned the number for Sanderson (S216) from the table; therefore, it was necessary to assign Emily Sanderson's book the preceding number from the table, that is, S215. To maintain a strict alphabetical order Mary Ellen Sanderson's book must be placed between the other two and therefore it was necessary to add a fourth digit to S215. Thus, by adding 5 to the work by Mary Ellen Sanderson there are now eight numbers left vacant for subsequent publications on general chemistry written by authors whose last names are Sanderson, namely, S2151, S2152, S2153, S2154, S2156, S2157, S2158, and S2159. If later the library were to acquire a general chemistry book by Alice Sanderson it would be necessary to assign it the number S214. But, if the number S214 had already been assigned to a book on general chemistry by Sandelmann then Alice Sanderson's book would be given the number S2145, thus maintaining an alphabetical order by author. In the same way, if at the time that Emily Sanderson's book was acquired the number S215 had already been assigned to a book by Sanders than Emily's number would have been S2155 and Mary Ellen's would have been assigned S2158. It is very unlikely that most libraries would ever have to resort to the use of four digits for the book number, but in specialized libraries or very large general ones it could happen occasionally.

Every author should be assigned only one book number under each classification number, but the same author will not necessarily have the same book number assigned to other works with different classification numbers.

Examples (in the order in which they were received and classified):

```
973          Baldwin, Dorothy May
B181             The American nation : a history of
                 the United States.

970          Baldwin, Leland Dewitt
B181             The story of the Americas : the
                 discovery, settlement, and develop-
                 ment of the new world.

973          Baldwin, Leland Dewitt
B182             The stream of American history.
```

A book number never represents any aspect of a publication or anyone connected with its production that is already indicated by the classification number. In those cases where a specific classification number is assigned to the works of a particular author (e.g., William Shakespeare, see chapter 11) or to a particular title (e.g., Beowulf or the Bible, see chapter 10), the main entry is never used as a base for forming the book number. In these cases some other factor concerning the publication is used, such as title, version, editor, annotator, translator, and so forth.

There are books for which it is more practical and logical to use the subject to form the book numbers rather than the main entry. Such is the method used to subarrange individual biographies, biographies of a family, and genealogies. (See chapter 9.) The subject is used to form the book number for commentaries and criticisms of the works of literary authors, musicians, painters, and other creative artists. In cases of reproductions of an artist's works where the main entry is not the artist, the name of the artist would be the most appropriate factor to use in the formation of the book number. A bibliography of the works by and/or about a person is given a book number corresponding to the subject and not the compiler of the bibliography. Indexes and concordances of a work or works of an author also will have book numbers based on the name of the author, and not on the name of the person who compiled the index or concordance. (See chapter 8.)

Examples:

```
016.370924    King, Clyde S.
M281              Horace Mann, 1796-1859 : a bibliography.

016.5         Miller, Marjorie M.
A832              Isaac Asimov : a checklist of works
                  published in the United States.

016.94205     Brushfield, Thomas Nadauld
R163              A bibliography of Sir Walter Raleigh.

520.924       Wright, Helen
M682              Sweeper of the sky : the life of
                  Maria Mitchell, first woman
                  astronomer in America.

759.13        Amon Carter Museum of Western Art.
O41               Georgia O'Keeffe : an exhibition of
                  the work of the artist from 1915 to 1966.

759.13        Matthews, Marcia M.
T166              Henry Ossawa Tanner : American artist.

793.320924    Biemiller, Ruth
D917              Dance : the story of Katherine Dunham.

910.924       Haslip, Joan
S786              Lady Hester Stanhope : a biography.
```

Work Marks

The work mark, or the title mark as it is sometimes called, consists of a letter (or letters) which represents the title of the work. This is appended to the author number from the Cutter-Sanborn table and always written in small letters, that is, lowercase or minuscule letters. The work mark is used only in those cases where the library acquires two or more books by the same author which are assigned the same classification number, making it necessary to distinguish between the different works. No work mark is necessary for the first (and in most cases this will be the only one) work of an author, but the second and all successive works must be assigned a work mark consisting of the initial letter of the first word of the title that is not an article.

Examples:

```
370.1        Conant, James Bryant
C743             Education for a classless society.

373.1        Conant, James Bryant
C743             The comprehensive high school : a second
                 report to interested citizens.

373.73       Conant, James Bryant
C743             The child, the parent and the state.

373.73       Conant, James Bryant
C743r            The revolutionary transformation
                 of the American high School.

378.73       Conant, James Bryant
C743             The citadel of learning.
```

To assign a work mark for works published with different titles or variations thereof, the title which has been established as the uniform title should be used. For information on determining uniform titles, consult the cataloging code.

When the library receives its first work of a prolific author and it is probable that the library will acquire more of the author's works which will be assigned the same classification number, this first work should be given a work mark. For further details on the use of work marks for the works of prolific authors see chapter 8.

Examples:

```
813.3      Irving, Washington
I72r           Rip Van Winkle : a legend of
               the Kaatskill  Mountains.


813.3      Irving, Washington
I72r           Rip Van Winkle : a tale of
B894           the Hudson.  Illustrated by
               Frances Brundage.


813.3      Irving, Washington
I72r           [Rip Van Winkle]
R122           The tale of Rip Van Winkle.
               With drawings by Arthur Rackham.


813.4      Melville, Herman
M531m          [Moby Dick]
               The whale.


813.52     Hemingway, Ernest
H488s          [The sun also rises]
               Fiesta.


823.5      Defoe, Daniel
D314m          [Moll Flanders]
A311           The life and adventures of Moll Flanders.
               Edited by George A. Aitken.


823.5      Defoe, Daniel
D314m          Moll Flanders.  With biographical
D257           note and introduction by W. H. Davies.


823.5      Defoe, Daniel
D314m          [Moll Flanders]
L225           The life and adventures of the famous
               Moll Flanders.  With drawings by
               Nigel Lambourne.


823.8      Dickens, Charles
D548d          [David Copperfield]
               The personal history of David Copperfield.
```

```
839.8226        Ibsen, Henrik
I14d                [A doll's house]
                    Nora : a play.    Translated by H. F.  Lord.


851.1           Dante Alighieri
D192d               [Divine comedy]
                    The vision, or Hell, Purgatory,
                    or Paradise.  Translated by W. H. Cary.


863.3           Cervantes Saavedra, Miguel de
C419d               [Don Quixote]
                    The history of Don Quixote.
                    Translated by John Ormsby.
```

Work marks will need to consist of two letters if the author has written two or more books classified under the same number and having titles beginning with the same letter of the alphabet. This second letter of the work mark may be: (1) another letter of the first word of the title, (2) the initial letter of the second word, or (3) the initial letter of a key word in the title. The following examples are arranged in the order in which the books were published and classified.

Examples:

```
813.54          Buck, Pearl S.
B922p               The patriot.   (1939)

813.54          Buck, Pearl S.
B922pr              The promise.  (1943)

813.54          Buck, Pearl S.
B922po              Portrait of a marriage.   (1945)

813.54          Buck, Pearl S.
B922pa              Pavilion of women.   (1946)

813.54          Buck, Pearl S.
B922pe              Peony.  (1948)
```

Some authors write series of books whose titles begin with the same words and for those works another key word or the first distinctive word of the titles should be used to form the work marks.

Examples:

```
811.4           Dunbar, Paul Laurence
D899c               Chris-mus is a comin', & other poems.

811.4           Dunbar, Paul Laurence
D899ℓh              Lyrics of the hearthside.

811.4           Dunbar, Paul Laurence
D899ℓs              Lyrics of sunshine and shadow.
```

811.4 D899ℓv	Dunbar, Paul Laurence Lyrics of love and laughter.
811.4 D899ℓw	Dunbar, Paul Laurence Lyrics of lowly life.
811.4 D899p	Dunbar, Paul Laurence Poems of cabin and field.
813.52 D816c	DuBois, Theodora The case of the perfumed mouse.
813.52 D816dc	DuBois, Theodora Death comes to tea.
813.52 D816dd	DuBois, Theodora Death dines out.
813.52 D816dt	DuBois, Theodora Death tears a comic strip.
813.52 D816f	DuBois, Theodora Face of hate.
813.52 D816fo	DuBois, Theodora Fowl play.
813.52 D816w	DuBois, Theodora Wild duck murders.

It is not necessary to add a letter to the book number of most books because few authors publish more than one book which have the same classification number.

Works Related to
Previous Publications

Works related to previous publications such as supplements, teacher's editions, indexes, concordances, commentaries, criticisms, condensations, abridgments, annotated versions, should be shelved with the works to which they are companionate. (For translations see chapter 7; for literary works and publications related to them see chapter 8.) It is necessary that works related to those previously published be given the same basic call number with an added mark or indication so that the related works follow the original on the shelves.

For supplements, teacher's editions, or indexes written either by the author of the original or by someone else, the only necessary addition to the call number is an indication such as supp. 1, supp. 2, teach.ed., or index. Examples:

```
016.815      Ireland, Norma Olin
I65              An index to monologs and dialogs.  1949.


016.815      Ireland, Norma Olin
I65              An index to monologs and dialogs.
supp. 1          A supplement.


296.125      Talmud.
S698             The Babylonian Talmud.  Translated into
                 English... under the editorship of
                 I. Epstein.  London: Soncino Press, 1935-48.


296.125      Slotki, Judah J.
S698             Index volume to the Soncino Talmud.
index            Compiled by Judah J. Slotki.
```

```
513          Morton, Robert Lee
M891             Making sure of arithmetic.


513          Morton, Robert Lee
M891             Making sure of arithmetic.
teach. ed.       Teacher's edition.


792.0942     Chambers, Edmund K.
C444             The Elizabethan stage.


792.0942     White, Beatrice
C444             An index compiled by Beatrice White,
index            to "The Elizabethan stage."
```

For criticisms, commentaries, and other related works the letter z is added to the work mark so that the writings about a specific work will follow the original and its translations. These publications will also need a second cutter number placed below the call number of the original work to represent the main entry of the related work.

Examples:

```
230.2        Thomas Aquinas, Saint
T463su           The Summa Theologica.


230.2        Garrigou-Lagrange, Reginald
T463suz          The Trinity and God the Creator :
G241             a commentary on St. Thomas'
                 Theological Summa.


230.2        Smith, Elwood F.
T463suz          A guidebook to the Summa.
S646


320.1        Machiavelli, Niccolo
M149p            The prince.  Reprinted from the
D119             translation of Edward Dacres.


320.1        Machiavelli, Niccolo
M149p            The prince.  Translated by
M359             W. K. Marriott.


320.1        Machiavelli, Niccolo
M149p            [Prince.  Italian]
Z613             Il principe.  Introduzione e
                 note de Federico Chabod.


320.1        Gilbert, Allan H.
M149pz           Machiavelli's Prince and its
G464             forerunners : The prince as a
                 typical book de regimine principum.


320.1        Sobel, Robert
M149pz           Niccolo Machiavelli's The Prince...
S677
```

370.1 R864e	Rousseau, Jean Jacques Emilius, or, A treatise on education.

370.1
R864ez
P318
	Patterson, Sylvia W.
	    Rousseau's Emile, and early
	    children's literature.

539.752
C975r
	Curie, Marie
	    Radioactive substances. A translation
	    from the French of the classical thesis
	    presented to the Faculty of Sciences
	    in Paris.

539.752
C975r
Z411
	Curie, Marie
	    Recherches sur les substances
	    radioactives.

539.752
C975rz
K65
	Klickstein, Herbert S.
	    Marie Sklodowska Curie : Recherches sur
	    les substances radioactives : a
	    bio-bibliographical study.

575.0162
D228or
	Darwin, Charles
	    On the origin of species by means of
	    natural selection, or, The preservation
	    of favored races in the struggle for life.

575.0162
D228or
Z928
	Darwin, Charles
	    [Origin of species. Dutch]
	    Het onstaan der soorten door
	    natuurlijke teeltkens.

575.0162
D228orz
B724
	A Book that shook the world : anniversary
	    essays on Charles Darwin's Origin of
	    species, by Julian S. Huxley and others.

575.0162
D228orz
E45
	Ellegard, Alvar
	    Darwin and the general reader : the
	    reception of Darwin's theory of evolution
	    in the British periodical press, 1859-1872.

Special Elements of the Call Number

Often it is necessary to add other elements to the call number which cannot be given as part of the book number. These are always written on the line below the number taken from the Cutter-Sanborn table.

The most common example of this is when it is necessary to distinguish between the various editions of a work. The year of publication of the second and subsequent editions should always form part of the call number. For the first edition it is not necessary to indicate the year of publication as most books never have more than one edition. The year of publication is used as an immediate indication of the currentness, obsolescence, or historical value of the item. The number of the edition alone has no relevance to any of these factors.

Examples:

```
709              Gardner, Helen
G227                 Art through the ages.  1926.

709              Gardner, Helen
G227                 Art through the ages.  Revised
1936                 edition.  1936.

709              Gardner, Helen
G227                 Art through the ages.
1948                 3d edition.  1948.

709              Gardner, Helen
G227                 Art through the ages.
1958                 4th edition.  1958.

770.28           Walls, Henry James
W215                 Photo-technique, fundamentals
                     and equipment.  1954.

770.28           Walls, Henry James
W215                 Camera techniques, fundamentals
1960                 and equipment.  2d edition.  1960.

770.28           Walls, Henry James
W215                 Camera techniques, fundamentals and
1964                 equipment.  3d revised edition.  1964.
```

For those works published in volumes, parts, fascicules, or other divisions or installments, each physical piece is marked with the appropriate indication, for example, v.1; v.2; v.3; pt. 1; pt. 2; fas. 1; fas. 2. This indicator should appear immediately below the author number on the spine of each physical piece, the book pocket, and the card used for circulation record, but never on the catalog cards.

Examples:

```
909          909          909
C432         C432         C432
v. 1         v. 2         v. 3


346.72       346.72       722.1        722.1
E75          E75          J34          J34
pt. 1        pt. 2        fas. 1       fas. 2
```

When a library has two or more copies of the same publication or any other item each copy is differentiated by copy numbers. Copy numbers can be appended to the call number and should always be the very last segment of the call number. The copy number must appear on the card used for the circulation record and the book pocket. Some libraries add the copy number to the call number on the spine of the book, but this is normally not considered necessary. Copy numbers never appear on the cards in the public catalog, but always are included on the shelflist card.

Examples:

```
025.3      025.3      025.3      653.1      653.1
M968       M968       M968       V642       V642
c. 1       c. 2       c. 3       c. 1       c. 2
```

Libraries using accession numbers to distinguish between the various copies should not use copy numbers.

Translations

The various editions of a work and the translations of that work into other languages should be shelved together. It is necessary to include as part of the call number a symbol that differentiates the various translations and at the same time keeps them in a logical order.[1] Many libraries whose collections are basically in English and whose clientele are mainly English-speaking prefer to treat all publications in foreign languages as though they were translations and give priority to the English version of all works. If the library has established the policy of using "uniform titles" in English, then the foreign language versions will be treated as though they were translations and the English version as the original. Libraries whose collections consist primarily of works in English should treat books in English as though they were the original.[2] Libraries acquiring books in various languages should follow the same policy for translations that has been established for the language of uniform titles.

To indicate that a publication is a translation (or in a language that is not English) another cutter number is added below the author's cutter number of the original edition. The following table is used to arrange the translations:

1. The basic purpose of a symbol for translations is to arrange these publications in a logical order and not to indicate in which language the work was originally published.

2. All examples given in this chapter and the succeeding ones treat all publications in English as though they were the originals and all publications in foreign languages are treated as translations.

Z2	English	Z6	Italian
Z3	Spanish	Z7	Portuguese
Z4	French	Z8	Russian
Z5	German	Z9	All other languages

The code Z1 is not used for translations. It is reserved for those instances in which an editor or annotator may have a last name which begins with letter Z.

In order to determine the symbol needed for translations the first two letters of the translator's surname are converted to digits using the following table and added to the code of the language into which the translation was made. For this code use the table given above. When a work is translated into a language which does not have its own code in the above table then Z9 is used and the first two letters of the name of the language are used instead of the translator's surname. A translation of a work into Spanish by Sanchez would have the mark Z371. Spanish is represented by Z3 and 71 stands for Sa of Sanchez. A work translated into Dutch would have the mark Z928. Z9 for "other languages" and 28 for Du of Dutch. This table for converting names of translators and languages is as follows:

A, B, C	=	1	P, Q[3], R	=	6
D, E, F	=	2	S, T	=	7
G, H, I	=	3	U, V, W	=	8
J, K, L	=	4	X, Y, Z	=	9
M, N, O	=	5			

If a library treats all versions in English as the original language and acquires a version of a book in the original language which would, of course, have no translator, the numbers 11 may be used, for example, a copy of Cervantes' *Don Quixote* in Spanish would have the number Z311. If the library has several versions or editions in the original language, the name of the editor, the version, the publisher, or any other name associated with the publication may be used in lieu of a translator's name.

Examples:

```
155.4      Montessori, Maria
M781           The secret of childhood.  Translated and
               edited by Barbara Barclay Carter.

155.4      Montessori, Maria
M781           [Secret of childhood.  Italian]
Z611           Il segreto dell'infanzia.
```

---

3. Always ignore the u that follows the q.

```
155.418      Mead, Margaret
M479             Culture and commitment : a study of the
                 generation gap.

155.418      Mead, Margaret
M479             [Culture and commitment.  French]
Z414             Le fosse des generations.  Traduit de
                 l'americain par Jean Clairevoye.

190          Russell, Bertrand
R961             Wisdom of the West : a historical survey
                 of Western philosophy in its social and
                 political setting.

190          Russell, Bertrand
R961             [Wisdom of the West. French]
Z471             L'aventure de la pensee occidentale.
                 Traduction de Claude Saunier.

193          Schopenhauer, Arthur
S373w            The world as will and idea.

193          Schopenhauer, Arthur
S373w            [World as will and idea.  German]
Z511             Die Welt als Wille und Vorstellung.

282.0924     Cabrini, Frances Xavier, Saint.
C117a            The travels of Mother Frances Xavier Cabrini...

282.0924     Cabrini, Frances Xavier, Saint.
C117a            [Travels of Mother Frances Xavier Cabrini. Italian]
Z675             Viaggi della Madre Francesca Xaverior Cabrini...
                 Torino: Societa editrice internazionale, 1922.

289.52       Eddy, Mary Baker
E21sc            Science and health, with key to the
                 Scriptures.

289.52       Eddy, Mary Baker
E21sc            [Science and health.  German]
Z577             Wissenschaft und Gesundheit, mit
                 Schlussel zur Helligen Schrift.
                 Boston: Allison V. Stewart, 1915.

301.023      Mead, Margaret
M479a            Anthropologists and what they do.

301.023      Mead, Margaret
M479a            [Anthropologists and what they do.  Spanish]
Z373             Antropología : la ciencia del hombre.
                 Buenos Aires: Ediciones Siglo Veinte, 1971.

306.8        Goldman, Emma
G619             Marriage and love.

306.8        Goldman, Emma
G619             [Marriage and love.  German]
Z555             Heirat und freie Liebe.  New York:
                 Mother Earth Publishing Company, 1917.
```

361.977311 A222t	Addams, Jane Twenty years at Hull House, with autobiographical notes.
361.977311 A222t Z558	Addams, Jane [Twenty years at Hull House. German] Zwanzig Jahre socialer Frauenarbeit in Chicago. Berechtigte Übersetzung von Else Munsterberg.
365.45 D261	Davis, Angela Y. If they come in the morning : voices of the resistance.
365.45 D261 Z411	Davis, Angela Y. [If they come in the morning. French] S'ils frappent a l'aube. Traduit de l'anglais par Rene Baldy.
365.45 D261 Z548	Davis, Angela Y. [If they come in the morning. German] Materialen zur Rassenjustiz : Stimmen des Wilderstands. Neuwied am Rhein: Luchterhand, 1972.
613.9 S225	Sanger, Margaret What every mother should know, or, How six little children were taught the truth
613.9 S225 Z551	Sanger, Margaret [What every mother should know. German] Was jede Mutter darf wisen. New York: Maisel, 1916.
720 W949w	Wright, Frank Lloyd Writings and buildings.
720 W949w Z545	Wright, Frank Lloyd [Writings and buildings. German] Schriften und Bauten. Ins Deutsche ubertragen von Peter Jones, Julia Knust und Theodor Knust.
910.02 S696	Somerville, Mary Physical geography.
910.02 S696 Z511	Somerville, Mary [Physical geography. German] Physische Geographie. Aus dem Englischen von Adolph Barth.
910.45 H615k	Heyerdahl, Thor Kon-Tiki : across the Pacific by raft. Translated by F. H. Lyon.
910.45 H615k Z362	Heyerdahl, Thor [Kon-Tiki. Spanish] Kon-Tiki : a través del Pacífico en una balsa. Versión española del Gen. Armando Revorado.

```
910.45       Heyerdahl, Thor
H615k           [Kon-Tiki.  French]
Z431            L'expedition du "Kon-Tiki" sur un radeau
                a travers le Pacifique.  Traduit de
                norvegien par Marguerite Gay.


910.45       Heyerdahl, Thor
H615k           [Kon-Tiki.  German]
Z542            Kon-Tiki : ein Floss treibt über den Pazifik.
                Ubersetzung von Karl Jettman.


910.45       Heyerdahl, Thor
H615k           [Kon-Tiki.  Portuguese]
Z755            A expedição Kon-Tiki : 8000 km. numa jangada
                atraves do Pacifico.  Tradução de Agenor
                Soares de Moura.


910.45       Heyerdahl, Thor
H615k           [Kon-Tiki.  Croatian]
Z916            Kon-Tiki : an splavi preko Tihog oceana.


910.45       Heyerdahl, Thor
H615k           [Kon-Tiki.  Dutch]
Z928            De Kon-Tiki expeditie : 8000 kilometre per
                vlot over de Grote Oceaan.  Geautoriseerde
                vertalig uit het noors van Amy van Marken.


910.45       Heyerdahl, Thor
H615k           [Kon-Tiki.  Norwegian]
Z955            Kon-Tiki ekspedisjonen.


910.45       Heyerdahl, Thor
H615k           [Kon-Tiki.  Polish]
Z965            Wy prawa Kon-Tiki.  Prezl.  z norweskiego
                Jerzy Panski.


910.45       Heyerdahl, Thor
H615k           [Kon-Tiki.  Swedish]
Z978            Expedition Kon-Tiki.  Oversattning...av
                Bengt Danielsson.


910.45       Duffs, Thomas A.
H615kz          Kon-Tiki, and Aku-Aku.
D857


944          Adams, Henry
A213            Mont-Saint Michel and Chartres.


944          Adams, Henry
A213            [Mont-Saint Michel and Chartres.  French]
Z426            Mont Saint Michel et Chartres, clefs du
                moyen-age français.  Traduit de l'anglais
                par Georges Fradier.


973.80924    Washington, Booker T.
W317            Up from slavery : an autobiography.
```

```
973.80924    Washington, Booker T.
W317            [Up from slavery.  Turkish]
Z978            Kölelikten kurtulus : bir tercümei hal.
                Tercüme eden Ayise Perter.
```

For examples of book numbers for translations of literary works see chapter 8.

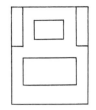

Literature and the Writings of Prolific Authors

It is necessary to have special guidelines for the works of literary authors and other prolific writers in different fields of knowledge. Each work by an author should be together with its various translations, versions, and editions. Also, commentaries and criticisms should be shelved with the original work.

The *Dewey decimal classification* makes no provision to maintain all the literary production of one author together; instead, the literary works of an author are divided according to the literary form (or genre), for example, poetry, drama, essays, fiction (novels and short stories), and so forth. Libraries usually classify a publication containing works of one author written in two or more literary forms under the classification number of the predominant literary form in that publication. The complete works of an author which contain two or more literary forms are classified under the number for the literary form for which the author is best known. Collections of the works of an author in a single literary form should be classified with other works in that same literary form and subdivided according to the period in which the author wrote. Thus, the works of a single author are not classified together, but rather dispersed and grouped by literary form.

The object of the following plan is to place in a logical order all the works by and about prolific authors. This plan can also be adapted to arrange the publications by and about other types of creative artists such as painters, sculptors, architects, musicians, and so forth.

The following is the recommended arrangement for organizing the works of prolific authors:

1. Complete works in the original language and in translation. (Classify complete works under the number of the literary form for which the author is best known.)
2. Selected works, selections (passages), and quotations from various works in the original language and in translation. (Classify selected works in one literary form under the number of that literary form; classify selected works in two or more literary forms under the number of the literary form which predominates the publication, or under the number of the literary form for which the author is best known.)
3. Individual works, their various editions, versions, translations, commentaries, criticisms, and other works related to a particular work. (Classify individual works under the number of the appropriate literary form.)
4. Writings related to several works of an author (excluding biographies, commentries, and criticisms). Included here are bibliographies, concordances, indexes, dictionaries, lists of characters, and so forth. (Classify such related works under the number of the literary form for which the author is best known if they cover works in two or more literary forms; however, if they pertain only to a group of works in one literary form they are classified with the works of that literary form.)
5. Biographies, autobiographies, correspondence, and diaries of the author. (Classify under the number of the literary form for which the author is best known.)
6. Commentaries and criticisms of the author's work. (Classify commentaries and criticisms of an author's work in general under the number of the literary form for which the author is best known: however, if the commentary or criticism is only concerned with an author's work in a particular literary form, then classify the publication under that form.)

The following sections of instructions and examples serve as guidelines for organizing the works of prolific authors in a systematic, logical, and practical manner.

Complete Works

An author number without any work mark is assigned to a publication containing the complete works of an author. If it is annotated or edited by someone other than the author then a second author number is placed below that of the author. Occasionally when editions are known by the name of the publisher, the publisher's name is used. If for some reason there is no name by which a particular edition can be identified and differentiated from all others, then the year of publication may be used and written below the author number. The first edition or publication of the complete works of an author need not have any other mark to distinguish it, but all succeeding ones must have one. For translations of complete works see chapter 7.

Examples:

811.1 W557	Wheatley, Phillis The poems of Phillis Wheatley, as they were originally published in London, 1773.
811.1 W557 M399	Wheatley, Phillis Poems. Edited, with an introduction by Julian D. Mason.
811.4 D899 H589	Dunbar, Paul Laurence [Works] The complete poems of Paul Laurence Dunbar, with the introduction to "Lyrics of lowly life," by W. D. Howells.
811.5 L914	Lowell, Amy [Poems] Complete poetical works.
813.4 T969 A512	Twain, Mark [Works] The complete works of Mark Twain. American artists edition.
813.4 T969 A939	Twain, Mark [Works] The writings of Mark Twain. Author's national edition.
813.4 T969 S885	Twain, Mark [Works] Writings of Mark Twain. Stormfield edition.
813.5 C363	Cather, Willa [Works] The novels and stories of Willa Cather.
821.1 C496 P771	Chaucer, Geoffrey Works. Edited by Alfred W. Pollard.
821.1 C496 R659	Chaucer, Geoffrey [Works] The complete works of Geoffrey Chaucer. Edited by F. W. Robinson.
821.1 C496 S627	Chaucer, Geoffrey [Works] The student's Chaucer, being a complete edition of his works. Edited from numerous manuscripts by the Rev. Walter M. Skeat.

```
822.8      Wilde, Oscar
W672           [Works]
               Complete works of Oscar Wilde.
```

Selected Works

This section includes not only selected works, but also selections (passages) and quotations from various works. The letter a is appended to the cutter number in order to place these publications immediately following those of complete works of the author. Below the author's cutter number another cutter number is added which represents the name of the compiler or editor. If there is no compiler or editor the name of the publisher or the year of publication may be used. For translations of selected works and selections see chapter 7.

Examples:

```
811.52     Cullen, Countee
C967a          [Selections]
               On these I stand : an anthology of the best
               poems of Countee Cullen, selected by himself...

811.52     DuBois, W. E. B.
D816a          [Poems]
G411           Selected poems.  Accra : Ghana
               University Press, 1964.

811.52     Hughes, Langston
H893a          [Poems]
               Selected poems by Langston Hughes.

811.52     Hughes, Langston
H893a          [Poems]
H794           Don't you turn back : poems.
               Selected by Lee Bennett Hopkins.

811.52     Hughes, Langston
H893a          [Poems.  Spanish]
Z331           Poemas. Versión castellana de Julio Galer.

811.52     Hughes, Langston
H893a          [Poems.  Portuguese]
Z751           Poemas de Langston Hughes.  Seleção,
               tradução e notas de Eduardo Martini.

811.52     McKay, Claude
M153a          [Poems]
C778           The dialect poetry of Claude McKay.  With
               a preface to this edition by Wayne Cooper.

811.52     McKay, Claude
M153a          [Poems]
E13            Selected poems of Claude McKay.  With a
               biographical note by Max Eastman.
```

```
812.52      Hughes, Langston
H893a           [Plays]
S635            Five plays.  Edited with an
                introduction by Webster Smalley.


812.52      Stein, Gertrude
S819a           [Plays]
V284            Last operas and plays.  Edited and with
                an introduction by Carl Van Vechten.


812.54      Hansberry, Lorraine
H249a           [Plays]
N434            Les blancs : the collected last plays of
                Lorraine Hansberry.  Edited with critical
                backgrounds by Robert Nemiroff.


813.4       Jewett, Sarah Orne
J59a            [Short stories]
C363            The best stories of Sarah Orne Jewett.
                Selected and arranged with a preface
                by Willa Cather.


813.52      Stein, Gertrude
S819a           [Selections]
V284            Selected writings of Gertrude Stein.
                Edited with an introduction by
                Carl Van Vechten.


813.54      Welty, Eudora
W464a           [Short stories]
V225            Thirteen stories.  Selected and with
                an introduction by Ruth M. Vande Kieft.


841.8       Rimbaud, Arthur
R575a           [Selections]
A141            Some poems of Rimbaud.  Translated by
                Lionel Abel.


841.8       Verlaine, Paul Marie
V521a           [Selections]
W769            Poems.  Selected and translated with an
                introduction by Ashmore Wingate.


843.9       Proust, Marcel
P968a           [Selections]
P343            Selections from Marcel Proust.  With
                introduction and notes by V. Payen-Payne,
                and a glossary.


861.42      Mistral, Gabriela
M678a           [Selections]
D167            Selected poems of Gabriela Mistral.
                Translated and edited by Doris Dana.


861.42      Mistral, Gabriela
M678a           [Selections.  Spanish]
Z311            Selección de poesías, por Gabriela
                Mistral.
```

```
861.42      Mistral, Gabriela
M678a           [Selections.  French]
Z451            Poemes choisis.  Traduction par
                Mathilde Pomes.


861.62      García Lorca, Federico
G216a           [Poems.  Spanish]
Z391            Antología.  Selección y
                prólogo de María F. Zambrano.
```

Individual Works

The individual works of an author in the same literary form are arranged alphabetically by title. A work mark consisting of one or two letters representing the title is appended to the cutter number of the author (see chapter 5). The work mark consisting of just the letter a has already been assigned to selected works and selections, therefore no work mark which consists of that single letter can be used for an individual work. Thus, all titles which begin with the letter a will require a work mark consisting of two letters, for example, aa, ab, ac, ad, and so forth. Also, the work marks zx, zy, and zz are reserved for other publications, and are explained below. Thus, work marks for individual works can range from aa to zw, using one or two letters as each case may require. If there are various editions of an individual title a second cutter number representing the editor, annotator, or publisher can be used; the year of publication could be used if there is no name which would be appropriate for the publication being classified, or if the year of publication would seem more pertinent. For translations of individual works see chapter 7.

The letter z is attached to the work mark to indicate a commentary or criticism of that particular individual work. Below the first cutter number representing the author, another cutter number is added which represents the person responsible (or the main entry) for the criticism or commentary.

The purpose of work marks is to maintain an alphabetical order of the individual works of an author with the following subarrangement:

1. The work in the original language (or in English), subarranged by year of publication or editor.
2. Versions in translation (or in foreign languages), subarranged by the name of the language.
3. Commentaries and criticisms about the work, subarranged by the author of the commentary or critic.

Examples:

```
811.52      Hughes, Langston
H893d           The dream keeper and other poems.
```

```
811.54        Brooks, Gwendolyn
B873r              Reckonings.

811.54        Brooks, Gwendolyn
B873ri             Riot.

811.54        Sanchez, Sonia
S211i              It's a new day : poems for young
                   brothas and sistuhs.

811.54        Sanchez, Sonia
S211w              We a baddDDD people.

812.54        Hansberry, Lorraine
H249r              A raisin in the sun : a drama in three acts.

812.54        Williams, Tennessee
W727g              The glass menagerie.

812.54        Williams, Tennessee
W727g              [Glass menagerie.  Spanish]
Z353               El zoológico de cristal.  Traducción
                   de León Mirlas.

812.54        Williams, Tennessee
W727g              [Glass menagerie.  Catalan]
Z911               Figuretes de vidre : comedia en dos
                   actes.  Versió de B. Vallespinosa.

812.54        Rathbun, Gilbert L.
W727gz             Tennessee Williams' The glass
R234               menagerie.

812.54        Williams, Tennessee
W727st             A streetcar named desire.

812.54        Williams, Tennessee
W727su             Summer and smoke.

813.4         Stowe, Harriet Beecher
S892u              Uncle Tom's cabin, or, Life
                   among the lowly.

813.4         Stowe, Harriet Beecher
S892u              [Uncle Tom's cabin.  Swedish]
Z978               Onkel Toms stuga.  Ofversättning at
                   Jean Rossander.

813.4         Friends of the Detroit Public Library.
S892uz             Uncle Tom's cabin as book and legend :
F911               a guide to an exhibition.

813.52        Wright, Richard
W952n              Native son.  New York: Harper, 1940.

813.52        Wright, Richard
W952n              Native son.  New York: Modern
M689               Library, 1942.
```

```
813.52      Wright, Richard
W952n           Native son.  With an introduction
O97             by William A. Owens.

813.52      Wright, Richard
W952n           [Native son.  Norwegian]
Z955            Nigger : roman.  Overs. av Johan Borgen.

813.52      Twentieth century interpretations of
W952nz          Native son : a collection of critical
T969            essays.  Edited by Houston A. Baker, Jr.

813.54      Purdy, James
P985n           The nephew.

823.912     Hall, Radclyffe
H178w           The well of loneliness.  With a
                commentary by Havelock Ellis.

823.912     Woolf, Virginia
W913m           Mrs. Dalloway.

823.912     Gilbert, Sandra M.
W913mz          Virginia Woolf's Mrs. Dalloway and
                To the lighthouse : a critical commentary.

823.914     Christie, Agatha
C555s           [So many steps to death]
                Destination unknown.
                London: Collins, 1954.

823.914     Christie, Agatha
C555s           So many steps to death.
1955            New York: Dodd, Mead, 1955.

823.914     Renault, Mary
R396c           The charioteer.

823,914     Renault, Mary
R396k           The king must die.

823.914     Renault, Mary
R396k           [The king must die.  German]
Z571            Der König müss sterben : roman.
                Deutsch von N. O. Scarpi.

823.914     Renault, Mary
R396ℓ           The last of the wine.

895.631     Murasaki, Shikibu
M972            The tale of Genji : a novel in six
                parts by Lady Murasaki.  Translated
                from the Japanese by Arthur Waley.
```

Writings Related to an Author's Work

The letters zx are appended to the cutter number of the author for such works as bibliographies by and about the author, dictionaries, concordances, lists of characters, indexes, and so forth. A cutter number representing the main entry is placed immediately below the cutter number of the author whose works are treated in the publication. The use of the letters zx arranges these types of publications in their appropriate order with all other works by and about the author.

Examples:

```
811.4        Clendenning, Shelia T.
D553zx           Emily Dickinson : a bibliography,
C627             1850-1966.

811.4        Rosenbaum, Stanford Patrick
D553zx           A concordance to the poems of
R813             Emily Dickinson.

811.52       Yost, Karl
M645zx           A bibliography of the works of
Y65              Edna St. Vincent Millay.

812.52       University of Texas.  Library.
H477zx           The Lillian Hellman collection
U58              at the University of Texas.

813.52       Lathrop, Jo Anna
C363zx           Willa Cather : a checklist of her
L354             published writings.

813.52       Kelly, William W.
G548zx           Ellen Glasgow : a bibliography.
K29

823.7        Chapman, Robert William
A933zx           Jane Austen : a critical bibliography.
C466

823.912      Kirkpatrick, Brownlee Jean
F733zx           A bibliography of E. M. Forster.
K59

823.912      Harmon, Robert Bartlett
S274zx           An annotated guide to the works
H288             of Dorothy L. Sayers.
```

Biographies, Autobiographies, Correspondence, and Diaries

The letters zy are appended to the cutter number of the author to indicate biographical materials about the author. A cutter number for the biographer is written below the one representing the biographee. The numbers A111 to A119 are used for autobiographies, correspondence, and diaries. Thus, all autobiographical material is together and shelved in front of the biographies written by others.

Examples:

```
811.1      Wheatley, Phillis
W557zy        [Correspondence]
A111          Letters of Phillis Wheatley,
              the Negro-slave poet of Boston.


811.1      Borland, Kathryn
W557zy        Phillis Wheatley : young
B735          Colonial poet.


811.1      DuBois, Shirley Graham
W557zy        The story of Phillis Wheatley :
D816          poetess of the American revolution.


811.52     Hughes, Langston
H893zy        The big sea : an autobiography.
A111


811.52     Meltzer, Milton
H893zy        Langston Hughes : a biography.
M528


813.4      Jewett, Sarah Orne
J59zy         [Correspondence]
A111          Letters.  Edited with an introduction
              by Richard Cary.


813.4      Thorp, Margaret F.
J59zy         Sarah Orne Jewett.
T517


813.52     Stein, Gertrude
S819zy        On our way, by Gertrude Stein &
A111          Alice B. Toklas.


813.52     Brinnin, John Malcolm
S819zy        The third rose : Gertrude Stein
B858          and her world.


813.52     Wright, Richard
W952zy        Black boy : a record of
A111          childhood and youth.


813.52     Bakish, David
W952zy        Richard Wright.
B168


813.52     Rickels, Milton
W952zy        Richard Wright, by Milton
R539          and Patricia Rickels.


813.52     Webb, Constance
W952zy        Richard Wright : a biography.
W365


813.54     Nance, William L.
C246zy        The worlds of Truman Capote.
N176
```

```
823.8          Bentley, Phyllis Eleanor
B869zy             The Bronte sisters.
B477


823.8          Hanson, Lawrence
B869zy             The four Brontes : the lives and works of
H251               Charlotte, Branwell, Emily and Anne Bronte.


823.912        Troubridge, Una Elena
H178zy             The life and death of Radclyffe Hall.
T859


839.81372      Migel, Parmenia
D583zy             Titania : the biography of
M634               Isak Dinesen.


841.8          Verlaine, Paul Marie
V521zy             [Correspondence]
A111               Lettres inédites á Charles Morice.
                   Publiées et annotées par Georges Zayed.


843.912        Gide, André
G453zy             [Correspondence]
A111               André Gide-Paul Valery : correspondence,
                   1890-1942.  Preface et notes par Robert Mallet.


895.635        Scott-Stokes, Henry
M678zy             The life and death of Yukio Mishima.
S431
```

Commentaries and Criticisms

The letters zz are added to the cutter number of the author for commentaries, criticisms, and analyses of the author's work in general, or of several of his works. Below this number is written a cutter number representing the main entry of the publication containing the commentary or criticism.
Examples:

```
811.52         Petitt, Jean Morris
M645zz             Edna St. Vincent Millay : a critical study
P491               of her poetry in its social and literary milieu.


812.54         Nelson, Benjamin
W727zz             Review notes and study guide to the major
N424               plays of Tennessee Williams.


813.52         Fabre, Michel
W952zz             The unfinished quest of Richard Wright.
F123               Translated from the French by Isabel Barzun.


813.52         Kinnamon, Kenneth
W952zz             The emergence of Richard Wright : a study
K55                in literature and society.
```

```
813.52      Richard Wright : impressions and perspectives.
W952zz          Edited by David Ray and Robert M. Farnsworth.
R511


813.54      Alexander, Charlotte A.
B181zz          Baldwin's Go tell it on the mountain,
A375            Another country, and other works : a
                critical commentary.


813.54      Bishop, Ferman
J59zz           The sense of the past in Sarah Orne Jewett.
B622


823.912     Bennett, Joan
W913zz          Virginia Woolf : her art as a novelist.
B471


823.912     Schaefer, Josephine O'Brien
W913zz          The three-fold nature of reality in the
S294            novels of Virginia Woolf.


839.81372   Langbaum, Robert Woodrow
D583zz          The gayety of vision : a study of
L271            Isak Dinesen's art.


841.8       Turnell, Martin
B338zz          Baudelaire : a study of his poetry.
T944


884.01      Robinson, David Moore
S241zz          Sappho and her influence.
R659
```

The following lists are comprehensive examples to illustrate the application of author numbers and work marks to various types of works by and about prolific authors.

```
WALT WHITMAN

811.3       Whitman, Walt
W615            [Works]
                The complete writings of Walt Whitman.


811.3       Whitman, Walt
W615            [Works]
D285            The complete poetry and prose of Walt Whitman,
                as prepared by him for the Deathbed edition.


811.3       Whitman, Walt
W615a           [Selections]
B652            The best of Whitman.  Edited and with an
                introduction and notes by Harold W. Blodgett.
```

```
811.3        Whitman, Walt
W615a            [Selections]
L917                 The tenderest lover : the erotic poetry of
                     Walt Whitman.  Edited and with an intro-
                     duction by Walter Lowenfels.

811.3        Whitman, Walt
W615a            [Selections]
S584                 Walt Whitman, poet of American democracy :
                     selections from his poetry and prose.  Edited
                     and with an introduction by Samuel Sillen.

811.3        Whitman, Walt
W615a            [Selections.  Spanish]
Z391                 Obras escogidas : ensayo biograficocrítico.
                     Versión, notas y bibliografía de Concha Zardoya

811.3        Whitman, Walt
W615a            [Selections.  French]
Z415                 Walt Whitman : choix des textes & traduction
                     par Helene Bokanowski.

811.3        Whitman, Walt
W615ℓ            Leaves of grass.  With an introduction by
A425             Bay Wilson Allen.

811.3        Whitman, Walt
W615ℓ            Leaves of grass.  With wood-engravings
H243             by Boyd Hanna.

811.3        Whitman, Walt
W615ℓ            [Leaves of grass]
W728                 The illustrated Leaves of grass.
                     Introduction by William Carlos Williams.

811.3        Whitman, Walt
W615ℓ            [Leaves of grass.  Spanish]
Z314             Hojas de hierba.  Versión...por
                 Francisco Alexander.

811.3        Whitman, Walt
W615ℓ            [Leaves of grass.  French]
Z417             Feuilles d'herbe.  Introduction et
                 traduction de Roger Asselineau.

811.3        Whitman, Walt
W615ℓ            [Leaves of grass.  Italian]
Z633             Foglie d'erba.  Versioni e
                 prefazione di Enzo Giachino.

811.3        Chandler, Thomas
W615ℓz           Walt Whitman's Leaves of grass.
C456

811.3        Miller, James Edwin
W615ℓz           A critical guide to Leaves of grass.
M648
```

```
811.3        Ogilvie, John Thayer
W615lz            The art of Leaves of grass : a cultural analysis
O34               of the final text with particular attention to
                  imagery, symbolism, and structure.


811.3        Whitman, Walt
W615o             O captain! My captain!


811.3        Whitman, Walt
W615s             Song of myself.


811.3        Whitman, Walt
W615s             [Song of myself.  Spanish]
Z322              Canto a mi mismo.  Traducción y prólogo
                  de León Felipe.


811.3        Eby, Edwin Harold
W615zx            A concordance of Walt Whitman's Leaves of
E16               grass and selected prose writings.


811.3        Wells, Carolyn
W615zx            A concise bibliography of the works of
W453              Walt Whitman, with a supplement of
                  fifty books about Whitman.


811.3        Whitman, Walt
W615zy            Correspondence.  Edited by Edwin
A111              Haviland Miller.


811.3        Briggs, Arthur E.
W615zy            Walt Whitman : thinker and artist.
B854


811.3        Holloway, Emory
W615zy            Free and lonesome heart : the secret
H745              of Walt Whitman.


811.3        A century of Whitman criticism.  Compiled
W615zz            by Edwin Haviland Miller.
C397


811.3        De Selincourt, Basil
W615zz            Walt Whitman : a critical study.
D457


811.3        Miller, Edwin Haviland
W615zz            Walt Whitman's poetry : a
M647              psychological journey.
```

GEORGE ELIOT

```
823.8        Eliot, George
E42               [Works]
1876              Novels of George Eliot.  New York: Harper, 1876.
```

```
823.8          Eliot, George
E42                Works. Bibliophile edition.
B582


823.8          Eliot, George
E42                [Works]
H226               The complete works of George Eliot.  With
                   photogravure illustrations from new drawings
                   by Gertrude Demain Hammond.


823.8          Eliot, George
E42                Works.  University edition.
U58


823.8          Eliot, George
E42a               [Selections]
M212               Child-sketches from George Eliot : glimpses
                   at the boys and girls in the romances of
                   the great novelist, by Julia Magruder.


823.8          Eliot, George
E42a               [Selections]
M689               The best known novels of George Eliot.
                   New York: Modern Library, 1940.


823.8          Eliot, George
E42a               [Selections]
S549               Character readings from "George Eliot."
                   Selected and arranged by Nathan Sheppard.


823.8          Eliot, George
E42h               How Lisa loved the king.


823.8          Eliot, George
E42md              Middlemarch : a study of provincial life.
1908               London: J. M. Dent, 1908.


823.8          Hardy, Barbara
E42mdz             Middlemarch : critical approaches to the novel.
H268


823.8          Smaridge, Norah
E42mdz             George Eliot : Middlemarch.
S636


823.8          Eliot, George
E42mf              The mill on the Floss.
1903               Edinburgh: Blackwood, 1903.


823.8          Eliot, George
E42mf              The mill on the Floss.  Edited with
A932               introduction and notes by Ida Ausherman.


823.8          Eliot, George
E42mf              The mill on the Floss.  New York: Dutton,
D979               1932.


823.8          Eliot, George
E42mf              The mill on the Floss.  Edited by
H427               Mary Sully Hayward.
```

823.8   Eliot, George
E42mf   [Mill on the Floss. Spanish]
Z363   El molino a orillas del Floss. Traducción
              del inglés por Vicente P. Quintero.

823.8   Eliot, George
E42mf   [Mill on the Floss. German]
Z526   Die Muhle am Floss. Ubersetzt
              von Julius Frese.

823.8   Casey, Floyd W.
E42mfz   Review notes and study guide to George
C338   Eliot's The mill on the Floss.

823.8   Good, Kathleen M.
E42mfz   George Eliot : The mill on the Floss.
G646

823.8   Eliot, George
E42sa   The sad fortunes of the Rev. Amos Barton.
1883   New York: M. L. Munro, 1883.

823.8   Eliot, George
E42sa   [Sad fortunes of Amos Barton. Danish]
Z921   Amos Bartons sorgelige Skaebne.
              Oversat af J. V. Osterberg.

823.8   Eliot, George
E42sc   Scenes of clerical life.
1887   New York: Harper, 1877.

823.8   Eliot, George
E42si   Silas Marner : the weaver of Raveloe.
1928   New York: Macmillan, 1928.

823.8   Eliot, George
E42si   Silas Marner : the weaver of Raveloe.
B617   With illustrations by Reginald Birch.

823.8   Eliot, George
E42si   Silas Marner. Illustrated by Percy Tarrant.
T192

823.8   Eliot, George
E42si   Silas Marner. Edited with introduction
W822   and notes by R. Adelaide Witham.

823.8   Eliot, George
E42zy   [Correspondence]
A111   The letters of George Eliot, selected with
              an introduction by R. Brimley Johnson.

823.8   Eliot, George
E42zy   [Correspondence]
A112   Letters from George Eliot to Elma Stuart,
              1872-1880. Edited by Roland Stuart.

```
823.8        Eliot, George
E42zy            [Correspondence]
A113             George Eliot's life as related in her letters
                 and journals.  Arranged and edited by her
                 husband, J. W. Cross.


823.8        Haight, Gordon Sherman
E42zy            George Eliot : a biography.
H149


823.8        Hardy, Barbara
E42zz            The novels of George Eliot : a study
H268             in form.


823.8        O'Brien, Kate
E42zz            George Eliot : a moralizing novelist.
O13


823.8        Stump, Reva Juanita
E42zz            Vision as imagery, theme, and structure
S934             in George Eliot's novels.
```

Biographies, Autobiographies, and Genealogies

The cutter number for individual biographies represents the name of the biographee, and not the name of the biographer. A letter is appended to the cutter number of the biographee which represents the biographer, albeit a person or a corporate body. This letter has the same function as a work mark which stands for a title and is appended to an author number. The letter a is reserved for autobiographical materials, thus for biographers whose last names begin with the letter A, two letters will have to be used (see the following paragraph). When there are two or more biographers whose last names begin with the same letter, two letters are used to differentiate between them. This is comparable to the work marks used to arrange and differentiate the works of authors which are classified under the same number and whose titles begin with the same letter. (See chapter 5.)

For autobiographies, correspondence, diaries, and other autobiographical materials the letter a is appended to the cutter number of the biographee and a second cutter number representing the editor, compiler, publisher, and so forth, is used to differentiate these materials. If there is only one autobiography a second cutter number may not be necessary. All biographies written by persons whose last names begin with A will need to have two letters appended to the cutter number representing the biographee. This use of "a" for autobiographical materials ensures that they will be shelved together and placed before all the biographical material about that person written by others.

Examples:

020.924 P989ℓ	Library of Congress. Herbert Putnam, 1861-1955 : a memorial tribute.
301.0924 M479a	Mead, Margaret Blackberry winter : my earlier years.
347.00924 H752a L616	Holmes, Oliver Wendell The mind and faith of Justice Holmes : his speeches, essays, letters, and judicial opinions. Selected and edited with intro- duction and commentary by Max Lerner.
347.00924 H752a M345	Holmes, Oliver Wendell The Holmes reader : the life, writings, speeches, constitutional decisions, etc. ...Selected and edited by Julius J. Marke.
347.00924 H752a S561	Holmes, Oliver Wendell Justice Oliver Wendell Holmes : his book notices and uncollected letters and papers. Edited and annotated by Harry C. Shriver.
347.00924 H752b	Bowen, Catherine Yankee from Olympus.
347.00924 H752h	Howe, Mark De Wolfe Justice Oliver Wendell Holmes.
347.00924 H752j	Judson, Clara Mr. Justice Holmes.
361.924 A222j	Judson, Clara City neighbor : the story of Jane Addams.
361.924 D619b	Baker, Rachel Angel of mercy : the story of Dorothea Lynde Dix.
520.924 B219d	DuBois, Shirley Graham Your most humble servant : the story of Benjamin Banneker.
610.730924 N687h	Harmelink, Barbara Florence Nightingale : founder of modern nursing.
613.90924 S225d	Douglas, Emily Taft Margaret Sanger : pioneer of the future.
730.924 H827a	Hosmer, Harriet Harriet Hosmer : letters and memories. Edited by Cornelia Carr.
759.13 C343s	Sweet, Frederick Arnold Miss Mary Cassatt : impressionist from Pennsylvania.
784.0924 A548a	Anderson, Marian My Lord, what a morning : an autobiography.

784.0924 A548a*l*	Albus, Harry James The 'Deep River' girl : the life of Marian Anderson in story form.
784.0924 A548sp	Spivey, Lenore Singing heart : a story based on the life of Marian Anderson.
784.0924 A548st	Stevenson, Janet Marian Anderson : singing to the world.
784.0924 K62a	Kitt, Eartha Thursday's child.
792.0924 W329a	Waters, Ethel His eye is on the sparrow : an autobiography.
796.3570924 M474a E35	Mays, Willie Born to play ball, as told to Charles Einstein.
796.3570924 M474a E36	Mays, Willie My life in and out of baseball, as told to Charles Einstein.
796.3570924 M474e	Einstein, Charles Willie Mays : coast to coast Giant.
796.3570924 M474h	Hano, Arnold Willie Mays.
796.3570924 M474ha	Hano, Arnold Willie Mays : the say-hey kid.
796.3570924 M474*l*	Liss, Howard The Willie Mays album.
796.3570924 M474sc	Schoor, Gene Willie Mays : modest champion.
796.3570924 M474sh	Shapiro, Milton J. The Willie Mays story.
796.3570924 M474sm	Smith, Ken The Willie Mays story.
796.3570924 R662r	Rowan, Carl Thomas Wait till next year : the life story of Jackie Robinson.
973.40924 S119b	Blassingame, Wyatt Sacagawea : Indian guide.
973.40924 S119f	Farnsworth, Frances Joyce Winged moccasins : the story of Sacajawea.
973.40924 S119fr	Frazier, Neta Sacajawea : the girl nobody knows.

```
973.40924      Seibert, Jerry
S119s               Sacajawea : guide to Lewis and Clark.

973.40924      Seymour, Flora Warren
S119se              Sacagawea : bird girl.

973.40924      Voight, Virginia Frances
S119v               Sacajawea.

973.40924      Waldo, Anne Lee
S119w               Sacajawea.

973.560924     Black Hawk, Sauk chief.
B628a               Black Hawk (Ma-ka-tai-me-she-kia-kiak) :
                    an autobiography.  Edited by Donald Johnson

973.560924     Cleven, Catherine Seward
B628c               Black Hawk : young Sauk warrior.

973.80924      Gehm, Katherine
W776g               Sarah Winnemucca : most extraordinary
                    woman of the Paiute nation.
```

Publications containing biographies of several persons are treated like any other publication, but genealogies and the biographies of members of the same family are treated as individual biographies, for example, the Wright brothers, Pierre and Marie Curie, Franklin and Eleanor Roosevelt, the Brontes.

Examples:

```
332.0924       Manchester, William Raymond
R682m               A Rockefeller portrait from John D. to Nelson.

332.0924       Morris, Joe Alex
R682mo              Those Rockefeller brothers : an informal
                    biography of five extraordinary young men.

332.0924       Silverberg, Robert
R682s               The fabulous Rockefellers : a compelling,
                    personalized account of one of America's
                    first families.

340.0922       Macdonell, Sir John
M135                Great jurists of the world.

510.922        Stoker, Frances Benson
S874                Famous mathematicians.

540.924        Rubin, Elizabeth
C975r               The Curies and radium.

550.922        Fenton, Carroll Lane
F342                The story of the great geologists.

551.4600922    Cox, Donald William
C877                Explorers of the deep : pioneers of oceanography.
```

```
629.1300924    Reynolds, Quentin Jones
W954r               The Wright brothers : pioneers of
                    American aviation.

730.922         Casson, Stanley
C345                XXth century sculptors.

792.0280924     Alpert, Hollis
B281aℓ              The Barrymores.

920.72          Strong, Joanna
S923                A treasury of the world's heroines.

929.2           Murphy, Anne Jacobs
B791m               History and genealogy of the Boykin family.

929.2           Brossman, Schuyler
M648b               The family of John Miller, 1858-1934 and
                    wife Kate S. Miller, 1862-1935.

973.90924       Churchill, Allen
R781c               The Roosevelts : American aristocrats.

973.90924       Hagedorn, Hermann
R781h               The Roosevelts of Sagamore Hill.
```

Many school and public libraries do not classify biographies with the specific discipline or subject area; instead they group them together under the letter B or the number 92, and then subarrange them alphabetically by biographee. In this case the same principles would apply, except that B or 92 would be used instead of the classification number.
Examples:

```
     B             B             B             B
   B118          C719b         C719p         C719pr

     B             B             B             B
   H632          N472          Y84f          Y84t
```

Some libraries prefer to use the entire last name of the biographee instead of a cutter number.
Examples:

```
   B        B         B          B          B          B
 Adams    Carver   Chisholm   Emerson   Rodriguez   White
```

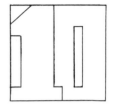

Anonymous Classics

An anonymous classic is a work of unknown or doubtful authorship which has appeared over the years in many editions, versions and/or translations, and which also has a uniform title used as the main entry. The most common types of anonymous classics are: poems, epics, romances, plays, chronicles, folk literature, sacred writings, and collections of ancient and medieval writings.

For the purposes of assigning book numbers anonymous classics can be divided into two principal categories: (1) those that are classified under a number in the *Dewey decimal classification* which represents a subject and not a particular title, and (2) works that have been given their own individual classification numbers in the *Dewey decimal classification*.

Most anonymous classics do not have their own individual classification numbers and for these works it is necessary to assign a cutter number that corresponds to the main entry, that is, the uniform title which has been established for that particular work. To distinguish the various editions and versions of such works a letter (or letters) representing the editor, translator, the name of the edition, or the publisher is appended to the cutter number. If none of these would be appropriate, then the year of publication may be used and written below the cutter number. The letters zy are added to the cutter number to indicate versions in foreign languages and a cutter number corresponding to the name of the language is placed below the number representing the uniform title. Commentaries, criticisms, and other writings about an anonymous classic have the letters zz appended to the cutter number and

below this is placed another cutter number corresponding to the last name of
the commentator, critic, or the main entry.

Examples:

342.73
F293
1937
	The Federalist.
	    The Federalist, or, The new Constitution
	    by Alexander Hamilton, James Madison and
	    John Jay. New York: Dutton, 1937.

342.73
F293m
	The Federalist.
	    The Federalist : a commentary on the
	    Constitution of the United States...
	    New York: Modern Library, 1941.

34 2.73
F293v
	The Federalist.
	    The Federalist, or, The new Constitution.
	    With an introduction by Carl Van Doren.

398.21
A658b
	Arabian nights.
	    The book of the thousand nights and a night.
	    Translated from the Arabic by Captain
	    Sir R. F. Burton.

398.21
A658h
	Arabian nights.
	    The Arabian nights entertainments.
	    With illustrations by William Harvey.

398.21
A658m
	Arabian nights.
	    The thousand and one nights, or, The
	    Arabian nights' entertainments.
	    Translated and arranged for family
	    reading by E. W. Miller.

398.21
A658zy
F873
	Arabian nights. French.
	    Les mille et une nuits : contes arabes.
	    Traduits par A. Galland.

398.21
A658zy
G373
	Arabian nights. German.
	    Tausend und eine Nacht, aus dem arabischen
	    übertragen von Max Henning.

398.21
A658zy
S735
	Arabian nights. Spanish.
	    El libro de las mil y una noches.
	    Versión español de Vicente Blasco-Ibañez.

398.21
A658zy
S736
	Arabian nights. Spanish.
	    Las mil y una noches : cuentos orientales.
	    Traducción de Pedro Pedraza y Paez.

398.21
A658zy
S737
	Arabian nights. Spanish
	    Las mil y una noches. Cuentos ilustrados
	    por José Segrelles.

398.21
A658zz
G368
	Gerhardt, Mia Irene
	    The art of storytelling : a literary
	    study of the Thousand and one nights.

```
398.21      Hole, Richard
A658zz           Remarks  on  the  Arabian  nights'  entertainments.
H729

398.21      Cinderella.
C574s            Cinderella,  or,  The  little  glass  slipper.
                 Pictures  by  Hilda  Scott.

398.21      Cinderella.
C574w            Cinderella  and  the  little  glass  slipper.
                 New  York:  White  &  Allen,  1889.

398.23      Legend of Kawelo.
L511g            The  legend  of  Kawelo.   Translated  from  a
                 Hawaiian  text  by  Laura  C.  Green.

398.245     Reynard the Fox.
R459o            The  scandalous  adventures  of  Reynard  the
                 Fox.   A modern  American  version  by  Harry  J.  Owens.

398.8       Mother Goose.
M918a            The  very  young  Mother  Goose.
                 Illustrated  by  Margot  Austin.

398.8       Mother Goose.
M918g            Mother  Goose,  or,  The  old  nursery  rhymes.
                 Illustrated  by  Kate  Greenaway.

821.3       Seven sages.
S497             The  history  of  the  seven  wise  masters
                 of  Rome.   Containing  many  ingenious
                 and  entertaining  stories.

839.61      Volsunga saga.
V934m            Volsunga  saga  :  the  story  of  the  Volsungs
                 and  Niblungs.   Translated  by  William  Morris.
```

The anonymous classics having their own individual classification numbers form a very small group which can be subdivided into two subgroups: (1) works where no provision is made in the *Dewey decimal classification* schedules for commentaries and translations, thus necessitating a subarrangement made through the book number for these types of related publications, and (2) works where the *Dewey decimal classification* does provide specific numbers for commentaries and translations.

The works of the first group which do not have specific numbers for commentaries and translations are:

```
Book of Mormon      289.322

Tripitaka           294.382 - 294.3823

Vedas               294.59212-294.59215

Upanishads          294.59218
```

Ramayana	294.5922
Mahabharata	294.5923
Bhagavad Gita	294.5924
Puranas	294.5925
Dharmasastras	294.5926
Beowulf	829.3

It is not necessary to assign a cutter number for the uniform titles of these ten works because each has its own classification number. The publications that are classified under each are arranged into three groups: (1) editions in English, (2) versions in other languages, and (3) commentaries and criticisms. The editions in English are assigned a cutter number representing the editor, translator, name of the edition, publisher, or any other name associated with the edition in hand. Use the table for translations in Chapter 7 for versions in foreign languages, and place this Z number immediately below the classification number. Editors of editions in English whose surnames begin with Z are limited to the numbers Z111 to Z199, because Z2 to Z9 are used for translations. Commentaries and criticisms follow the versions in foreign languages; the cutter number for these is Z999 to which is appended a letter (or letters) representing the last name of the commentator or critic, in the same way that work marks are used for literature. (See chapter 5).

Examples:

289.322
C562
	Book of Mormon.
	    The Book of Mormon : an account written by the
	    hand of Mormon upon plates taken from the plates
	    of Nephi. Translated by Joseph Smith, jun.
	    Salt Lake City: Church of Jesus Christ of
	    Latter Day Saints, 1923.

289.322
C562
1943
	Book of Mormon.
	    The Book of Mormon : an account written by the
	    hand of Mormon upon plates taken from the plates
	    of Nephi. Translated by Joseph Smith, jun.
	    Salt Lake City: Church of Jesus Christ of
	    Latter Day Saints, 1943.

289.322
D451
	Book of Mormon.
	    The Book of Mormon...Translated by Joseph
	    Smith, jun. Salt Lake City: Deseret News, 1918.

289.322
D452
	Book of Mormon.
	    The Book of Mormon : an account written by the
	    hand of Mormon. Salt Lake City: Desert Sunday
	    School Union, 1915.

289.322
E13
	Book of Mormon.
	    The Book of Mormon...Translated by Joseph Smith,
	    Jr. Divisions into chapters & verse by Orson
	    Pratt. New York: Eastern States Mission, 1908.

289.322   Book of Mormon.
Z179   The Book of Mormon...Translated by Joseph Smith,
          jun. Independence, Missouri: Zion's Printing
          and Publishing Co., 1910.

289.322   Book of Mormon. French.
Z471   Le livre de Mormon : recit ecrit de la main
          de Mormon sur des plaques prises des plaques
          de Nephi. Traduit de l'anglais par John
          Taylor et Curtis E. Bolton.

289.322   Book of Mormon. Dutch.
Z928   Het boek van Mormon. Uit het Engelsch
          vertaald door J. W. F. Volker.

289.322   Budvarson, Arthur
Z999b   The Book of Mormon : true or false?

289.322   Reynolds, George
Z999r   Commentary on the Book of Mormon.

294.382   Tripitaka.
C454   The sutras of 42 sections and two other
          scriptures of the Mahayana school. Newly
          translated from the Chinese by Chu Chan.

294.382   Tripitaka.
M454   The lion's roar : an anthology of the
          Buddha's teachings selected from the Pali
          by David Maurice.

294.382   Tripitaka.
S968   The Tibetan Tripitaka. Edited by
          Daisetz T. Suzuki.

294.382   Woodward, Frank Lee
Z999w   Pali Tripitakam concordance, being a
          concordance in Pali to the Three baskets
          of Buddhist scriptures in the Indian
          order of letters.

294.59212 Vedas. Rigveda.
L551   Hymns from the Rig-Veda. Translation...
          by Jean LeMee.

294.59212 Vedas. Rigveda.
M136   Hymns from the Rigveda. Selected & metrically
          translated by A. M. Mcdonnell.

294.59212 Vedas. Rigveda. Spanish.
Z354   Los himnos mágicos del Rig-Veda.
          Traducido por Antonio del Olmo Ruíz.

294.59213 Vedas. Samaveda.
G854   The hymns of the Samaveda. Translated
          with a popular commentary by Ralph T. H.
          Griffith.

294.59218 M395	Upanishads. Himalayas of the soul. Translations from the Sanskrit of the principal Upanishads, by J. Mascaro.
294.59218 N692	Upanishads. The Upanishads. Translated from the Sanskrit...by Swami Nikhilananda.
294.59218 Z965	Upanishads. Polish. Upaniszady. Przelozyl z sanskrytu Stanislaw Fr. Michaelski-Iwienski.
294.59218 Z999p	Pandit, Madhav Pundalik The Upanishads : gateways of knowledge.
294.5922 D979	Ramayana. Ramayana : the epic of Rama, prince of India. Condensed into English verse by Romesh Dutt.
294.5923 A753	Mahabharata. Indian idylls from the Sanskrit by Edwin Arnold.
294.5923 D979	Mahabharata. Mahabharata : the epic of ancient India. Condensed into English verse by Romesh Dutt.
294.5923 Z421	Mahabharata. Le Maha-bharata : poeme epique de Krishna- Dwaipayana...Traduit...du sanskrit en français par Hippolyte Fauche.
294.5923 Z935	Mahabharata. Indonesian. Mahabharata. Disusun dan di-Indonesiakan oleh Usman Effendi.
294.5923 Z999sh	Sharma, Ram Karan Elements of poetry in the Mababharata.
294.5923 Z999so	Sorenson, Soren An index to the names in the Mahabharata, with short explanations and a concordance to the Bombay and Calcutta editions.
294.5923 Z999su	Sukthankar, Vishnu Sitaram On the meaning of the Mahabharata.
294.5924 M952	Bhagavadgita. The song divine, or, The Bhagavad Gita, by Dhan Gopal Muherji.
294.5924 T455	Bhagavadgita. The song of the Lord : Bhagavadgita. Translated with introduction by Edward J. Thomas.

294.5924
Z999b
	Barborka, Geoffrey A.
	    The pearl of the Orient : the message of
	    the Bhagavad-Gita for the Western World.

294.5924 Z999bo	Bonnerjee, Jitendriya The Gita : the song supreme.
294.5924 Z999g	Ghose, Aurobindo Essays on the Gita.

294.5924
Z999f
	Faucett, Lawrence William
	    Seeking Krishna in his teachings : an
	    analytical arrangement of the Bhagavad Gita.

294.5925
K18
	Puranas.
	    The Puranic anthology. Edited by A. P.
	    Karmakar, with a foreword by B. N. Datar.

829.3
L581
	Beowulf.
	    Beowulf. Translated into verse by
	    William Ellery Leonard.

829.3
M877
	Beowulf.
	    Tale of Beowulf. Translated by William
	    Morris and A. J. Wyatt.

829.3
Z415
	Beowulf. French.
	    Beowulf : epopée anglo-saxonne. Traduite
	    en français...par L. Botkine.

829.3
Z955
	Beowulf. Norwegian.
	    Beowulf og Striden um Finnsberg. Fra
	    angelsaksisk ved Henrik Rytter.

829.3
Z999s
	Storms, Godfrid
	    Compounded names of people in Beowulf :
	    a study in the diction of a great poet.

There are four collections of writings that have their own classification numbers as well as specific numbers for translations and commentaries. These are all religious writings and are:

Bible and its parts, including apocryphal books.	220 - 229

Talmud, including talmudic
    literature and other
    related writings.
	296.12 - 296.19

Koran and its suras.	297.122 - 297.1229
Hadith, writings on Islamic traditions.	297.124 - 297.1248

An edition of one of these four works or of any of its parts is assigned a cutter number representing the version, translation, or any other name related to the publication in hand. It is not necessary to assign a cutter number to indicate the language, or to separate the criticisms and interpretations because the *Dewey decimal classification* provides specific numbers for these types of publications. However, it should be noted that there are five English versions of the Bible which have their own classification numbers, namely, Douay (220.5202); Authorized, or King James (220.5203); Revised, or American revised (220.5204); Confraternity (220.5205); and the New English Bible (220.5206). For these five versions whose classification numbers already indicate the main entry, version, and language it is necessary to use some other name for their subarrangement, such as editor, publisher, illustrator, or any other name related to the publication.

Examples:

```
220.5202    Bible.  Douay.  1955.
O18             The Holy Bible; Old Testament in the
                Douay-Challoner text; New Testament and
                Psalms in the Confraternity text.
                Edited by John P. O'Connell.

220.5203    Bible.  Authorized.  1970.
H747            The Holy Bible, containing the Old and New
                Testaments.  Authorized King James version...
                Philadelphia: A. J. Holman Co., 1970.

220.5203    Bible.  Authorized.  1971.
L425            The Christian worker's Bible.  Authorized
                King James version.  Edited by J. Gilchrist
                Lawson and Jesse Lyman Hurlbut.

220.5203    Bible.  Authorized.  1961.
N277            The Holy Bible, containing the Old and
                New Testaments...commonly known as the
                authorized King James version.  Phila-
                delphia: National Bible Press, 1961.

220.5203    Bible.  Authorized.  1952.
W927            The Holy Bible, containing the Old and
                New Testaments...conformable to the
                edition of 1611, commonly known as the
                Authorized or King James version.  Cleveland:
                World Publishing Company, 1952.

220.5204    Bible.  Revised standard.  1953.
N431            The Holy Bible : revised standard version
                containing the Old and New Testaments...
                New York: T. Nelson, 1953.

220.5206    Bible.  New English.  1971.
C178            The New English Bible with the Apocrypha.
                New York: Cambridge University Press, 1971.
```

220.531   Bible. German. Riessler-Storr, 1956.
R562   Die Heilige Schrift des alten und neuen
                    Bundes. Übersetzt von Paul Riessler und
                    Rupert Storr.

220.541   Bible. French. Maredsous. 1949.
M324   La Sainte Bible. Version nouvelle d'apres
                    les textes originaux par les mains de
                    Maredsous.

220.561   Bible. Spanish. Torres Amat. 1958.
T487   La Sagrada Biblia. Traducida de la vulgate
                    latina al español por Felix Torres Amat.

220.6   Childs, Brevard S.
C537   Myth and reality in the Old Testament.

220.7   Clarke, Adam
C597   Commentary on the Holy Bible.

220.7   Henry, Matthew
H523   Commentary on the whole Bible, Genesis
                    to Revelation.

221.052   Bible. O.T. Douay. 1975.
D726   The Old Testament faithfully translated
                    into English by the English College of Douai.

221.6   Smart, James D.
S636   The Old Testament in dialogue with modern man.

221.7   Harrelson, Walter J.
H296   Interpreting the Old Testament.

222.106   Suelzer, Alexa
S944   The Pentateuch : a study in salvation history.

222.1107   Kidner, Derek
K46   Genesis : an introduction and commentary.

222.35   Bible. O.T. Ruth. 1971.
S296   The book of Ruth. Illustrated by
                    Jacob Schaham.

223.2   Bible. O.T. Psalms. Perowne. 1968.
P453   The book of Psalms : a new translation
                    with introduction and notes...by J. J.
                    Stewart Perowne.

223.206   Bible. O.T. Psalms XXIII. Authorized. 1970.
A581   The Twenty-third Psalm. King James version.
                    Illustrated by Marie Angel.

223.206   Elliott, Norman K.
E46   The Lord your shepherd : the Twenty-third
                    Psalm for modern man.

224.806   Watts, John D.
W351   Studying the book of Amos.

225.6   Ryan, Rosalie
R989   Contemporary New Testament studies.

226.052   Bible. N.T. Gospels. Christianson. 1973.
C555   The concise Gospel and the Acts. Compiled
                    by Christopher J. Christianson.

296.125   Talmud.
E64   The Babylonian Talmud. Translated into
                    English with notes, glossary, and indices
                    under the editorship of I. Epstein.

296.125   Talmud.
R692   New edition of the Babylonian Talmud.
                    Original text edited, corrected, formulated,
                    and translated into English by Michael
                    Rodkinson.

296.12506   Gold, Wolf
G618   Lessons in Talmud.

296.12507   Adler, Morris
A237   The world of the Talmud.

297.1225   Koran.
B435   The Quran. Translated...by Richard Bell.

297.1225   Koran.
S163   The Koran translated into English from
                    the original Arabic by George Sale.

297.122541   Koran. French.
M781   Le Coran. Traduction nouvelle par
                    Edouard Montet.

297.1226   Baljon, Johannes
B186   Modern Muslim Koran interpretation, 1880-1960.

297.1226   Bell, Richard
B435   Introduction to the Quran.

297.1226   O'Shaughnessy, Thomas
O82   The development of the meaning of spirit
                    in the Koran.

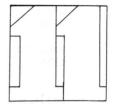

Authors with Individual Classification Numbers

There are three authors in the *Dewey decimal classification* who have been assigned their own classification numbers, namely, Caedmon (829.2), Cynewulf (829.4), and William Shakespeare (822.33).

Caedmon was an English poet of the seventh century, who is often referred to as the "Father of English poetry" because he is the first known poet to use English. Cynewulf was an Anglo-Saxon poet of the eighth century. Works by and about these two poets are assigned author numbers corresponding to the editor, translator, title, or any other name related to the work being classified.

Examples:

```
829.2        Caedmon.
K35               The Caedmon poems.  Translated into English
                  verse by Charles W. Kennedy.


829.2        Caedmon.
T518              Caedmon's metrical paraphrase of the Holy
                  Scriptures in Anglo-Saxon.  With an English
                  translation, notes, and a verbal index by
                  Benjamin Thorpe.


829.4        Cynewulf.
C555g             Cynewulf's Christ : an eighth century English
                  epic.  Edited with a modern rendering by
                  Israel Gollancz.
```

829.4 C555w	Cynewulf. The Christ of Cynewulf : a poem in three parts. Translated into English by Charles H. Whitman.
829.4 E39	Cynewulf. Elene : an old English poem. Edited with introduction, Latin original notes, and complete glossary by Charles W. Kent.
829.4 K35	Cynewulf. The poems of Cynewulf. Translated into English by Charles W. Kennedy.

Shakespeare wrote much and much has been written about Shakespeare; therefore it is necessary to have a special book number scheme to arrange the works by and about Shakespeare. The *Dewey decimal classification* does include a special plan for subarranging works by and about this English playwright, but it is inadequate for most libraries and does not provide a very logical or mnemonic subarrangement. Therefore the following plan is offered for those libraries desiring a practical, mnemonic, and logical arrangement of Shakespearian collections.

COMPLETE WORKS

A12   Complete works in English. Subarranged by editor,
           annotator, name of the edition or any other name
           related to the production of the publication in
           hand. If there is no name that would be appro-
           priate the year of publication may be used.

A123-A129 Complete works in other languages.

          A123 Spanish. Subarrange by translator.

          A124 French. Subarrange by translator.

          A125 German. Subarrange by translator.

          A126 Italian. Subarrange by translator.

          A127 Portuguese. Subarrange by translator.

          A128 Russian. Subarrange by translator.

          A129 Other languages. Subarrange by a cutter
                number representing the name of the
                language.

SELECTED WORKS

A13   Selected works. Use for collections of three or
           more works which cannot be classified under
           A21, A31, A41 and X22. Subarrange by editor,

selector, year of publication, or any name related to the publication in hand. Classify publications containing only two works under the first one mentioned on the title page. (See the Anglo-American cataloging code.)

A132   Selected works in English.

A133-A139   Selected works in other languages. Subdivide like A123-A129.

A14   Condensations and adaptations of three or more works which cannot be classified under A22, A32, or A42. Subarrange by adaptor, abridger, or any other appropriate name. Classify publications containing only two works under the first one mentioned on the title page. (See the Anglo-American cataloging code.)

A142   Condensations and adaptations in English.

A143-A149   Condensations and adaptations in other languages. Subdivide like A123-A129.

A15   Quotations and/or selected passages from various works which cannot be classified under A23, A33, or A43. Subarrange by editor, selector, or any other appropriate name.

A152   Quotations and/or selected passages in English.

A153-A159   Quotations and/or selected passages in other languages. Subdivide like A123-A129.

COMEDIES

All's well that ends well	Much ado about nothing
As you like it	Pericles
The comedy of errors	The taming of the shrew
Cymbeline	The tempest
Love's labor's lost	Troilus and Cressida
Measure for measure	Twelfth night
The merchant of Venice	The two gentlemen of Verona
The merry wives of Windsor	The winter's tale
A midsummer night's dream	

A21   Comedies. Use for collections of three or more comedies. Subarrange in the same manner as explained under A12. Classify publications

containing only two works under the first
one mentioned on the title page. (See the
Anglo-American cataloging code.)

A212   Comedies in English.

A213-219   Comedies in other languages.
                    Subdivide like A123-A129.

A22   Condensations and adaptations of three or more
                    comedies. Subarrange by adaptor, abridger,
                    or any other appropriate name. Classify
                    publications containing only two works under
                    the first one mentioned on the title page.
                    (See the Anglo-American cataloging code.)

A222   Condensations and adaptations of comedies in English.

A223-A229   Condensations and adaptations of comedies in other
                    languages. Subdivide like A123-A129.

A23   Quotations and/or selected passages from various
                    comedies. Subarrange by editor, selector,
                    or any other appropriate name.

A232   Quotations and/or selected passages from various
                    comedies in English.

A233-A239   Quotations and/or selected passages from various
                    comedies in other languages. Subdivide like
                    A123-A129.

            TRAGEDIES

Antony and Cleopatra   Macbeth

Coriolanus   Othello

Hamlet   Romeo and Juliet

Julius Caesar   Timon of Athens

King Lear   Titus Andronicus

A31   Tragedies. Use for collections of three or more
                    tragedies. Subarrange in the same manner
                    as explained under A12. Classify publications
                    containing only two works under the first
                    one mentioned on the title page. (See the
                    Anglo-American cataloging code.)

A312   Tragedies in English.

A313-A319   Tragedies in other languages.
                    Subdivide like A123-A129.

A32   Condensations and adaptations of three or more
             tragedies. Subarrange by adaptor, abridger,
             or any other appropriate name. Classify
             publications containing only two works under
             the first one mentioned on the title page.
             (See the Anglo-American cataloging code.)

A322   Condensations and adaptations of tragedies in
             English.

A323-A329   Condensations and adaptations of tragedies in
             other languages. Subdivide like A123-A129.

A33   Quotations and/or selected passages from various
             tragedies. Subarrange by editor, selector,
             or any other appropriate name.

A332   Quotations and/or selected passages in English.

A333-A339   Quotations and/or selected passages in other
             languages. Subdivide like A123-A129.

             HISTORIES

             Henry IV   King John

             Henry V   Richard II

             Henry VI   Richard III

             Henry VIII

A41   Histories. Use for collections of three or more
             histories. Subarrange in the same manner
             as explained under A12. Classify publications
             containing only two works under the first
             one mentioned on the title page. (See the
             Anglo-American cataloging code.)

A412   Histories in English.

A413-A419   Histories in other languages. Subdivide like A123-A129.

A42   Condensations and adaptations of three or more
             histories. Subarrange by adaptor, abridger,
             or any other appropriate name. Classify
             publications containing only two works under
             the first one mentioned on the title page.
             (See the Anglo-American cataloging code.)

A422   Condensations and adaptations of histories in
             English.

A423-A429   Condensations and adaptations of histories in
             other languages. Subdivide like A123-A129.

A43   Quotations and/or selected passages from various
             histories. Subarrange by editor, selector,
             or any other appropriate name.

A432   Quotations and/or selected passages in English.

A433-A439   Quotations and/or selected passages in other
                languages. Subdivide like A123-A129.

Individual Works

Each individual work has been assigned four basic consecutive cutter numbers which will arrange editions and versions of the texts and writings about them in a logical order. The first number is for editions and versions of the text; the second one for condensations and adaptations; the third for quotations and selected passages; the fourth number is assigned to commentaries, criticisms, and other related works such as bibliographies, concordances, and so forth. All titles are subdivided like the example given below for *All's well that ends well.*

A62-A65   All's well that ends well.

   A622   Editions and versions. Subarrange by editor,
                annotator, name of the edition, or any other
                name related to the production of the publica-
                tion in hand. If there is no name that would
                be appropriate the year of publication may
                be used.

   A623-A629   Translations into other languages. Subdivide
                like A123-A129. Subarrange by name of trans-
                lator or name of the language as explained
                under A123-A129.

   A63   Condensations or adaptations. Subarrange by
                adaptor or abridger, or any other appropriate
                name.

   A64   Quotations and/or selected passages. Subarrange
                by editor, selector, or any other appropriate
                name.

   A65   Commentaries, criticisms, bibliographies,
                concordances, and other such related works.
                Subarrange by main entry.

A72-A75   Antony and Cleopatra

A82-A85   As you like it

C22-C25   The comedy of errors

C32-C35   Coriolanus

C42-C45   Cymbeline

H12-H15   Hamlet

H22-H25	Henry IV, parts 1 and 2
H32-H35	Henry IV, part 1
H36-H39	Henry IV, part 2
H42-H45	Henry V
H62-H65	Henry VI, parts 1, 2, and 3
H72-H75	Henry VI, part 1
H82-H85	Henry VI, part 2
H85-H89	Henry VI, part 3
H92-H95	Henry VIII
J22-J25	Julius Caesar
K22-K25	King John
K32-K35	King Lear
L22-L25	Love's labor's lost
M22-M25	Macbeth
M32-M35	Measure for measure
M42-M45	The merchant of Venice
M52-M55	The merry wives of Windsor
M62-M65	A midsummer's night dream
M72-M75	Much ado about nothing
O22-O25	Othello
P22-P25	Pericles
	Poetical works
P32-P35	Complete poetical works
P42-P45	Sonnets
P52-P55	A lover's complaint
P62-P65	The passionate pilgrim
P72-P75	The phoenix and the turtle
P82-P85	The rape of Lucrece
P92-P95	Venus and Adonis

R22-R25   Richard II

R32-R35   Richard III

R42-R45   Romeo and Juliet

T22-T25   The taming of the shrew

T32-T35   The tempest

T42-T45   Timon of Athens

T52-T55   Titus Andronicus

T62-T65   Troilus and Cressida

T72-T75   Twelfth night

T82-T85   The two gentlemen of Verona

W22-W25   The winter's tale

SPURIOUS AND DOUBTFUL WORKS

X22   Writings attributed to Shakespeare, e.g., The two
       noble kinsmen; King Edward III; The booke of
       Sir Thomas Moore. Subarrange by title.

X23   Commentaries, criticisms, and theories about the
       works attributed to Shakespeare. Subarrange
       by main entry.

RELATED WORKS

Y22   Writings related to the works of Shakespeare, such
       as dictionaries, concordances, lists of
       characters of several plays, etc. Subarrange
       by main entry.

Y23   Writings related to the presentation of Shakespeare's
       plays, such as works about the Globe Theatre,
       actors, festivals, etc. Subarrange by main
       entry.

Y24   Bibliographies (including biobibliographies) of
       writings by and about Shakespeare. Subarrange
       by main entry.

Y25   Biographies and other works related to the life of
       Shakespeare. Subarrange by biographer.

COMMENTARIES AND CRITICISMS

Z22   Commentaries and criticisms of Shakespeare's work
       in general. Subarrange by main entry.

Z23	Commentaries and criticism of the comedies. Subarrange by main entry.
Z24	Commentaries and criticisms of the tragedies. Subarrange by main entry.
Z25	Commentaries and criticisms of the histories. Subarrange by main entry.

Examples:

822.33
A12
H319
	Shakespeare, William
	    [Works]
	    The complete works of Shakespeare.
	    Edited by G. B. Harrison.

822.33
A123
A859
	Shakespeare, William
	    [Works. Spanish]
	    Obras completas. Estudio preliminar,
	    traduccion y notas por Luis Astrana-Marin.

822.33
A124
F646
	Shakespeare, William
	    [Works. French]
	    Oeuvres completes. Avant-propos d'Andre Gide.
	    Introduction generale et textes de presentation
	    d'Henri Fluchere.

822.33
A125
S339
	Shakespeare, William
	    [Works. German]
	    Shakesperes werke in vierzehn teilen.
	    Ubersetzt von August Wilhelm von Schlegel.

822.33
A132
K62
	Shakespeare, William
	    [Selections]
	    Five plays of Shakespeare.
	    Edited by George L. Kittredge.

822.33
A132
S413
	Shakespeare, William
	    [Selections]
	    Four plays : Julius Caesar, Macbeth, As
	    you like it, Hamlet. Edited by H. C.
	    Schweikert.

822.33
A134
M623
	Shakespeare, William
	    [Selections. French]
	    Oeuvres choisies de Shakespeare.
	    Traduction revue par F. M. Michel.

822.33
A142
C967
	Cullum, Albert
	    Shake hands with Shakespeare : eight
	    plays for elementary schools.

822.33
A152
S611
	Shakespeare, William
	    [Selections]
	    Quotations from Shakespeare.
	    Selected by Gertrud Simonsson.

822.33   Shakespeare, William
A212   [Selections]
M689   The comedies of Shakespeare.
                  New York: Modern Library, 1943.

822.33   Shakespeare, William
A312   [Selections]
W954   Four great tragedies : Romeo and Juliet,
                  Julius Caesar, Hamlet, Macbeth. Edited
                  by William Aldin Wright.

822.33   Shakespeare, William
A412   [Selections]
M689   The histories of Shakespeare.
                  New York: Modern Library, 1947

822.33   Shakespeare, William
A822   As you like it. Edited by
B623   Isabel J. Bisson.

822.33   Shakespeare, William
A826   [As you like it. Italian]
L824   Come vi place. Traduzione di
                  Cesare Vico Lodovici.

822.33   Shakespeare, William
A83   As you like it : a radio adaptation
M847   by Brewster Morgan.

822.33   Culver, Mary Carol
A85   A study of the imagery in Shakespeare's
C968   As you like it.

822.33   Twentieth century interpretations of
A85   As you like it : a collection of critical
T971   essays, edited by Jay L. Halio.

822.33   Shakespeare, William
H122   Hamlet. Edited by
V517   A. W. Verity.

822.33   Shakespeare, William
H129   [Hamlet. Dutch]
D975   Het treurspel van Hamlet, prins van
                  Denemarken. Vertaald door Nico van Suchtelen

822.33   Raven, Anton Adolph
H15   A Hamlet bibliography and reference
R253   guide, 1877-1935.

822.33   Shakespeare, William
J222   Julius Caesar. Edited for school
G827   use by Margaret R. Grennan.

822.33   Shakespeare, William
J222   Julius Caesar. With an introduction and
R196   footnotes, and edited by V. K. Rangachari.

```
822.33        Shakespeare, William
J223              [Julius Caesar.  Spanish]
B191              Julio Cesar.  Prólogo, texto y traducción
                  por Rafael Ballester-Escalas.


822.33        Shakespeare, William
J224              [Julius Caesar.  French]
R362              Jules Cesar.  Adaptation par
                  Jean-François Reille.


822.33        Shakespeare, William
J225              [Julius Caesar.  German]
Z63               Julius Caesar.  In deutsche Sprache
                  übertragen von Theodor von Zeynek.


822.33        Shakespeare, William
J229              [Julius Caesar.  Danish]
D186              Julius Caesar : en tragedie af
                  William Shakespeare.  Oversat af H. Lasson.


822.33        Shakespeare, William
J229              [Julius Caesar.  Swedish]
S974              Julius Cesar : skadespel.  Ofversattning
                  af Georg Scheutz.


822.33        Shakespeare, William
P322              [Poems]
S594              Sonnets, songs, and poems.
                  Edited by Henry W. Simon.


822.33        Knight, George Wilson
P35               The mutual flame : on Shakespeare's
K69               Sonnets and The phoenix and the turtle.


822.33        Shakespeare, William
P422              [Sonnets]
1933              Shakespeare's sonnets.
                  New York: Harper, 1933.


822.33        Shakespeare, William
P424              [Sonnets.  French]
G236              Les sonnets.  Traduction de
                  Charles Marie Garnier.


822.33        Bertram, Paul Benjamin
X23               Shakespeare and The two noble kinsmen.
B548


822.33        Hubbell, Lindley Williams
X23               A note on the Shakespeare apocrypha.
H876


822.33        Kokeritz, Helge
Y22               Shakespeare's names : a pronouncing
K79               dictionary.


822.33        Spevack, Marvin
Y22               A complete and systematic concordance
S752              to the works of Shakespeare.
```

```
822.33      Thomson, Wilfrid Harry
Y22             Shakespeare's characters : a
T486            historical dictionary.

822.33      Davies, William Robertson
Y23             Shakespeare's boy actors.
D257


822.33      Shirley, Frances Ann
Y23             Shakespeare's use of
S558            off-stage sound.

822.33      Smith, Gordon Ross
Y24             A classified Shakespeare bibliography,
S648            1936-1958.

822.33      Harris, Frank
Y25             The man Shakespeare and his
H314            tragic life-story.

822.33      Reese, Max M.
Y25             Shakespeare : his world and his work.
R329


822.33      Wolff, Emil
Y25             Shakespeare : el problema de su
W855            personalidad y su obra.

822.33      Price, George R.
Z22             Reading Shakespeare's plays : a
P945            guide for college students.

822.33      Brown, John Russell
Z23             Shakespeare and his comedies.
B878


822.33      Ribner, Irving
Z24             Patterns in Shakespearean tragedy.
R485

822.33      Spurgeon, Caroline Frances Eleanor
Z24             Leading motives in the imagery of
S772            Shakespeare's tragedies.
```

Appendixes

1.   Bibliography of Cutter Author Number Tables

This list of the Cutter tables in chronological order is an attempt to identify and describe the different tables as they appeared. For some reason not a single version, edition, or reprinting of any Cutter table ever contained imprint information of any kind, except for the Swanson-Swift revisions of 1969. It seems incredible that such a prominent person in the field of cataloging and classification as Charles Ammi Cutter would allow such an important contribution to the field of librarianship to be published without a place of publication; a name of a publisher or a printer; or a date! For this reason, the imprints for all editions before 1969 are written in brackets.

These ten tables represent the basic editions and versions of the Cutter author number tables. There have been many reprintings of most of them, and in some cases the reprints contained corrections of typographical errors, and/or slight changes in the title information. However, these ten Cutter author number tables are distinctly differentiated because of their formats or the numbers assigned to different letter groups.

> [Cutter's decimal author table.] [Boston: 1880].
>> This was the original table sold by Cutter and announced in the September-October 1880 issue of *Library journal*. Because there is no known extant copy a description is impossible.
>
> [Alfabetic-order table. Boston: 1886?]. 2 pp. of tables. 28 x 28 cm.
>> This is the second two-figure table published approximately six years after Cutter began selling the preliminary version.

Alfabetic-order table. Rev. ed. [Boston: 1888]. 4 pp. of tables. 31 x 31 cm. This revised and expanded version of the two-figure table had a slight rearrangement of some of the letters, and the letters A, E, I, O, and S had more numbers assigned to them. The total quantity of numbers for the twenty-six letters was increased from 2,576 to 2,727. A few of the letter combinations also were assigned different numbers, but for the most part the table was very similar to the 1886 edition.

C. A. Cutter's alfabetic order table. Alternatives for the vowels and S (single initials to be used instead of the first two letters), by Miss Kate E. Sanborn. [Boston: Library Bureau, 1892]. 4 pp. of tables. 33 x 17 cm.

C. A. Cutter's alfabetic-order table—consonants, except S. Altered and fitted with three figures by Miss Kate E. Sanborn. [Boston: Library Bureau, 1895]. 14 p. of tables. 33 x 28 cm.

C. A. Cutter's alfabetic-order table—consonants, except S and vowels and S. Altered and fitted with three figures by Miss Kate E. Sanborn. [Boston: Library Bureau, 1896?]. 18 pp. of tables. 33 x 19. This table combined into one physical volume the consonants and vowels of the Cutter-Sanborn tables which were originally published in separate volumes.

C. A. Cutter's three-figure alfabetic-order table—consonants, except S and vowels and S. [Boston: Library Bureau, 1901]. 26 pp. of tables. 34 x 19 cm.

Cutter-Sanborn three-figure author table. Swanson-Swift revision, 1969. Chicopee, Mass.: H. R. Huntting Co., 1969. 33 pp. of tables. 39 x 22 cm.

C. A. Cutter's three-figure author table. Swanson-Swift revision, 1969. Chicopee, Mass.: H. R. Huntting Co., 1969. 29 pp. of tables. 39 x 29 cm.

C. A. Cutter's two-figure author table. Swanson-Swift revision, 1969. Chicopee, Mass.: H. R. Huntting Co., 1969. 4 pp. of tables. 36 x 22 cm.

2. A Substitute for a Cutter Author Number Table

If the library does not own a Cutter author number table and does not have the resources to purchase one, the following table may be used in its place. Use the initial letter of the author's name (or the first word that is not an article in the case of main entries which are titles or corporate names) and then convert the following three letters to numbers according to the table given below.

A, B, C	=	1	P, Q[1], R	=	6
D, E, F	=	2	S, T	=	7
G, H, I	=	3	U, V, W	=	8
J, K, L	=	4	X, Y, Z	=	9
M, N, O	=	5			

1. Always ignore the u that follows the q.

Examples:

Abramson	= A161
Currier	= C866
Fukuda	= F848
Larson	= L167
Mutual of Omaha	= M878
Quinlan	= Q354
Ray	= R19
Scribner	= S163
United States	= U537
Whitlock	= W337
Young	= Y585

Bibliography

The purpose of this chronologically arranged bibliography is to give a historical perspective of the most significant and influential literature about book numbers. The items are subarranged under each year chronologically by month. All the works listed in this bibliography were consulted by the author.

1876.

Poole, William Frederick. "The organization and management of public libraries." In *Public libraries in the United States of America: their history, condition, and management. Part I.* U.S. Bureau of Education, pp. 492–93. Washington: Government Printing Office, 1876.

Yates, James. [Public library systems of England.] *Library journal*, 1. (November 1876): 122–23.

1878.

Schwartz, Jacob. "A 'combined' system for arranging and numbering." *Library journal* 3 (March, 1878): 6–10.

Cutter, Charles Ammi. "Another plan for numbering books." *Library journal* 3 (September 1878): 248–51.

Schwartz, Jacob. "Mr. Cutter's numbering plan." *Library journal* 3 (October 1878): 302.

1879.

Dewey, Melvil. "Principles underlying numbering systems–first paper." *Library journal* 4 (January 1879): 7–10.

"Plans for numbering, with especial reference to fiction: a library sympo-sium." [Contributions by: John Edmands, Josephus N. Larned, Melvil Dewey, Charles A. Cutter, and Frederic B. Perkins.] *Library journal* 4 (February 1879): 38–47.

Edmands, John. "Proportion of initial letters in author catalogs." *Library journal* 4 (February 1879): 56.

Dewey, Melvil. "Principles underlying numbering systems—second paper: a new numbering base." *Library journal* 4 (March 1879): [75]–79.

————. "Arrangement on the shelves—first paper." *Library journal* 4 (April 1879): 117–20.

————. "Arrangement on the shelves—second paper." *Library journal* 4 (June 1879): 191–94.

1881.

Massey, A. P. "Classification of fiction." *Library journal* 6 (January 1881): 7–9.

1882.

Cutter, Charles Ammi. *Boston Athenaeum: How to get books, with an explanation of the new way of marking books*. Boston: Press of Rock-well and Churchill, 1882. pp. 14–18; 35–36.

Schwartz, Jacob. "A new classification and notation." *Library journal* 7 (July-August 1882): 148–66.

Fitzgerald, John. "Mnemonic numbering." *Library journal* 7 (September 1882): 229–30.

1883.

Lane, William Coolidge. [Plan adopted for Greek and Latin authors.] *Library journal* 9 (March 1884): 50–51.

Cutter, Charles Ammi. "Arrangement and notation for Shakesperiana." *Library journal* 9 (August 1884): 137–39.

1885.

Goddard, E. N. "Classification of fiction." *Library journal* 10 (March 1885): 55.

Biscoe, Walter Stanley. "Chronological arrangement on shelves." *Library journal* 10 (September-October 1885): 245–46.

Lane, William Coolidge. "Report on classification, 1883–85." *Library journal* 10 (September-October 1885): 257–61.

1886.

Swan, Charles H. "Alfab.-order table for names of places." *Library journal* 11 (April 1886): 118.

Cutter, Charles Ammi. "Author-tables for Greek and Latin authors." *Library journal* 11 (August-September 1886): 280–89.

Dewey, Melvil. "Eclectic book-numbers." *Library journal* 11 (August-September 1886): 296–301.

1887.

"Libraries on special authors." *Library notes* 2 (June 1887): 14–16.

Cutter, Charles Ammi. "How to use Cutter's decimal author table." *Library journal* 12 (July 1887): 251–52.

Cole, George Watson. "Some thoughts on close classification." *Library journal* 12 (September-October 1887): 360.

Cutter, Charles Ammi. "Cutter's author-table: the arrangement of biography." *Library journal* 12 (December 1887): 544.

_____. "Addendum [to] How to use Cutter's decimal author table." *Library journal* 12 (December 1887): 549.

1888.

Cutter, Charles Ammi. "Adversaria." *Library journal* 13 (March-April 1888):79.

"Cutter author-numbers in connection with the Dewey Classification: [a symposium]." *Library journal* 13 (September-October 1888): 308–9.

1893.

Cutter, Charles Ammi. "The Cutter author marks: why and how they are used." In his *Expansive classification. Part I*, pp. 139–60. Boston: The Author, 1891–1893.

Olin, C. R. "An order table for collective biography." *Library journal* 18 (May 1893): 144.

Richardson, Ernest Cushing. "An expansive author-table." *Library journal* 18 (June 1893): 187.

"Book numbers." *Library notes* 3 (October 1893): 419–50.

1896.

Langton, H. H. "Systems of shelf-notation." *Library journal* 21 (October 1896): 441–43.

Cutter, Charles Ammi. "Comment." *Library journal* 21 (October 1896): 443.

1899.

Cutter, Charles Ammi. *Explanation of the Cutter-Sanborn author-marks (three-figure tables)*. 3rd ed. Northampton, Mass.: Herald Office, 1899.

1901.

Ashley, Frederick W. "Size marks for class numbers." *Library journal* 26 (January 1901): 22.

Cutter, Charles Ammi. *Explanation of the alphabetic-order marks (three-figure tables)*. Northampton, Mass.: C. A. Pierce & Company, 1901.

1902.

Daniels, Joseph F. "Author and title marks in fiction." *Public libraries* 7 (April 1902): [143]–44.

Library of Congress. *Shelf list rules*. [Washington: Government Printing Office], 1902.

1904.

Cutter, Charles Ammi. *Explanation of the Cutter-Sanborn author-marks (three-figure tables)*. 4th ed., rev. by Kate Emery Jones. Boston: Library Bureau, 1904.

1910.

Bliss, Henry Evelyn. "Simplified book-notation." *Library journal* 35 (December 1910): 544–46.

1911.

Cutter, Charles Ammi. *Explanation of the alphabetic-order marks (two-figure tables)*. Northampton, Mass.: Herald Job Print., 1911.

Mead, H. Ralph. "Some problems in book numbers." *ALA bulletin* 5 (July 1911): 251–53.

1912.

Bliss, Henry Evelyn. "A simplified alphabetic-order table." *Library journal* 37 (February 1912): 71–74.

Merrill, William Stetson. "The Merrill book numbers." *Public libraries* 17 (April 1912): 127–29.

1917.

Andrews, C. W. "Principles of classification." *ALA bulletin* 11 (July 1917): 195–97.

Fletcher, William Isaac. "Some notes on classification." *ALA bulletin* 11 (July 1917): 340–41.

Laws, Anna Cantrell. *Author notation in the Library of Congress*. Washington: Government Printing Office, 1917.

1919.

Wiley, Edwin. "Some sidelights on classification." *Library journal* 44 (June 1919): p. 363.

University of Chicago Library. *Rules for shelflisting*. Chicago: University of Chicago Press, 1919.

1924.

Dewey, Melvil. "Temporary fads." *Library journal* 49 (January 1, 1924): 38.

1932.

Tomlinson, Anna Louise. "Are Cutter numbers doomed?" *Library journal* 57 (March 15, 1932): 292.

Brown, Zaidee. "More about Cutter numbers." *Library journal* 57 (May 1, 1932): 437.

1937.

Barden, Bertha R. *Book numbers: a manual for students with a basic code of rules*. Chicago: American Library Association, 1937.

1940.

Neiswanger, Laura. "Book numbers in university libraries." *Catalogers' and classifiers' yearbook*, no. 8, 1939. Chicago: American Library Association, 1940. pp. 88–95.

1955.

Mayol, Josefina. "Author numbers for Spanish names in the literature class." *Journal of cataloging & classification* 11 (July 1955): 138–43.

1962.

Málaga, Luis F. *Tablas de notación interna para bibliotecas hispánicas (de dos y tres cifras), con un código de reglas para su aplicación*. (Cuadernos bibliotecológicos, no. 7). Washington: Unión Panamericana, 1962.

1965.

Merryman, John Henry, and Long, Rosalee M. "A new author notation." *Library resources & technical services* 9 (Summer 1965): 356–58.

1969.

Swanson, Paul K., and Swift, Esther M. *Instruction book for C. A. Cutter's two-figure table*. Swanson-Swift revision, 1969. Chicopee, Mass.: H. R. Huntting Co., 1969.

——, and ——. *Instruction book for C. A. Cutter's three-figure table*. Swanson-Swift revision, 1969. Chicopee, Mass.: H. R. Huntting Co., 1969.

——, and ——. *Instruction book for Cutter-Sanborn three-figure author table*. Swanson-Swift revision, 1969. Chicopee, Mass.: H. R. Huntting Co., 1969.

Levy, Grace. "Cuttering the corporate entry." *Special libraries* 60 (December 1969): 657–58.

1975.

Lehnus, Donald J. *Signaturas librísticas: normas para su apliacación en bibliotecas de habla hispana.* Río Piedras, Puerto Rico: Editorial Universidad de Puerto Rico, 1975.

1977.

La Trobe University Library. Technical Services Division. *Book numbers guide.* (Library publications, no. 13) Bundoora, Australia: The Library, 1977.

1978.

Lehnus, Donald J. *Notação de autor: manual para bibliotecas.* Tradução e adaptação de Hagar Espanha Gomes. Rio de Janeiro: BNG/Brasilart, 1978.

Index

Designed by Vladimir Riechl
Composed by Modern Typographers, Inc.,
in Linotron 202 Times Roman
with Helvetica display type
Printed on 50# Glatfelter Antique,
a pH neutral stock,
and bound by Malloy Lithographing, Inc.

Designed by Vladimir Reichl
Composed by Modern Typographers, Inc.
in Linotron 202 Times Roman
with Helvetica display type
Printed on 50# Glatfelter, smooth
B 66 natural finish,
and bound by Maple-Vail Bookmanufacturing, Inc.